The Prairie Man

by
Steven Porter

Phantom Publications, Inc.

All Rights Reserved

The Prairie Man is a play in two acts requiring six main characters and a small number of additional players who represent the citizens of Illinois and Washington, D.C. The action takes place between 1831 and 1859 and concerns the life of Abraham Lincoln, particularly his relationship with Anne Rutledge of New Salem. Playing time is approximately two hours.

CAST OF CHARACTERS
(in order of appearance)

JOSHUA SPEED

ABRAHAM LINCOLN

ANN RUTLEDGE

SPEAKER of the Illinois Assembly

STEPHEN DOUGLAS

MARY TODD

CITIZENS of Illinois and Washington, D.C.

The Prairie Man was first performed on August 17, 1990 at the Helen Foley Theatre in Binghamton, New York with the following cast:

Joshua Speed	Steven Westlake
Abraham Lincoln	Jim Hull
Ann Rutledge	Kristin Gartner Hull
Stephen Douglas	Dale Robinson
Mary Todd	Elaine Kuracina Brehm

The production was directed by author Steven Porter. The Technical Director and Scenic Designer was Lawrence Kassan. The Wardrobe Director was Nancy Brietske.

Preface

Although ***The Prairie Man*** is a work of fiction, it deals with characters who really lived, characters who played an important role at a critical time in the history of America. For that reason, it may be useful to take a closer look at them and at how the play was written and originally produced. Let's start with the women.

Ann Rutledge. Ann was born in 1813, the daughter of James Rutledge, a co-founder of New Salem, Illinois where our play begins. She was one of nine children, described by Carl Sandburg in his three-volume biography of Lincoln as being delicately built, pretty, with auburn hair and blue eyes. John McNamar, one of Ann's suitors, added that her lips were cherry red, that she was a gentle, amiable maiden without the airs of city belles. In his book *The Lincoln Nobody Knows,* Richard Current quotes Lincoln's law partner, William Herndon, as saying that Ann stood 5'2", "blond with blue eyes, blessed with every feminine virtue and grace."

There is very little to tell us how Ann grew up, how she and Abe met, and how they formed their relationship. We do know that her father ran a tavern in New Salem, that she worked in the tavern, and that for a short time, Lincoln was a boarder there during his early days in the town. When the Rutledges moved to a farm some seven miles away, Lincoln is known to have been a visitor, often stopping to see Ann on his many trips as a surveyor.

The romance between Ann and Abe was apparently intertwined with Ann's suitor, John McNamar. McNamar was a business speculator who came to New Salem under the name of McNeil in 1832. He struck some deals with Ann's father which included a pledge to marry Ann as soon as he could settle some family affairs back home in New York. He wrote Ann from Ohio and again from New York but never returned to claim her. Sandburg concludes that eventually she released him from his pledge, and continued to build a relationship with Lincoln "who could hardly have been unaware of what she was going through."

It is difficult at best to accurately describe the nature of the relationship between Ann and Abe from 1832 to 1835 because we have no direct correspondence between them. Our data comes mostly from accounts given by Herndon and others many years after Ann's death. In Benjamin Thomas's book entitled *Abraham Lincoln,* Herndon is quoted as saying that the two were deeply in love, and that after Ann died, the memory of her, remaining forever within Abe, "was the source of much of his melancholy and also the inspiration for most of his greatness."

What we do know for sure was that Ann succumbed on August 25, 1835 during an outbreak of malaria and typhoid fever which swept through the town. Ironically, John McNamar returned to New Salem just three weeks later.

Mary Todd. In her own way, Mary Todd was a victim of history almost as tragic as her husband, though her life began in wealth and social prominence. She was born on December 13, 1818, the fourth child of Robert and Eliza Todd. The Todds had risen to the front ranks of Kentucky banking, and Mary was blessed with a comfortable home and a good education. Though her mother died when Mary was only six, her father remarried and the household regained its stability.

At the age of twenty-one, Mary went to Springfield, Illinois to live with her older sister, Elizabeth. Elizabeth had married Ninian Edwards, the son of the former Governor of Illinois, and thus it was into a politically and socially active environment that Mary was transplanted.

She adapted to it with relish and soon found herself courted by many of the leading figures of the city, among them Abraham Lincoln and Stephen Douglas. It is ironic that the political rivalry between Lincoln and Douglas should also express itself in the social parlors of Springfield, but there is little doubt that at the same time Lincoln pledged to marry her, Mary was engaged in a fairly serious flirtation with Douglas. Author Richard Current quotes a relative of Mary Todd as follows: "She loved Douglas, and but for her promise to marry Lincoln, would have accepted him." In fact, Mary became so sick over the matter that her physician was obliged to pay a visit to Douglas asking him to give up his pursuit of her—which he did.

As for Abe, Mary's conduct was so infuriating that he stood her up on their wedding day. It was only the intercession of Joshua Speed which saved the relationship...but more of that later.

Mary's stormy courtship with Lincoln was a harbinger of things to come. When finally they were married (November 4, 1842), it was not into a union of consummate harmony. To quote Paul Angle in his book *Mary Lincoln: wife and widow*, "The course of the marriage was not always smooth. Lincoln was reserved, introspective, and deficient in social graces, whereas his wife was vivacious, self-centered, and ambitious." She often spoke of him in derogatory terms, such as the time she was asked to describe their first meeting at a Springfield ball in 1839. "He wanted to dance with me in the worst way, and he certainly did."

Mary bore Abe four sons, only one of whom, Robert Todd, lived to maturity. Her second child, Edward, died in infancy, but it was the death of her third son, William, in 1862 which became the emotional watershed of her life. She was by then the First Lady and had already made many enemies in Washington with her acid tongue and meddlesome personality. But now she became increasingly more neurotic, and when she witnessed the murder of her husband at Ford's Theatre on April 15, 1865, the event drove her to a state of mental illness.

Following the assassination, Mary became obsessed with delusions of poverty, though she was quite comfortable on Lincoln's estate and an annual pension from Congress of $3000 (increased to $5000 in 1880). She even took to selling her own wardrobe, so great was her fear of financial ruin. For three years she lived in Chicago and then traveled extensively in Europe, returning to the US in 1871. Shortly thereafter, her youngest son, Thomas, died at age eighteen. It was for Mary the final emotional blow. By 1875 her mental illness was so acute that her son Robert brought insanity proceedings against her. On May 19, 1875 a jury found her legally insane, and she was remanded to an institution and later to the care of her sister in Springfield.

Even though a second jury in 1876 pronounced her sane once more, for all practical purposes she was never again normal. From 1876 to 1880, she lived in France, incessantly consumed with delusions of poverty, and when in 1880 she returned to her sister Elizabeth's care, she was in a state of mental and physical collapse. Mary died in Springfield on July 16, 1882.

Abraham Lincoln. There are very few who do not know the major events of Abe Lincoln's life: of his birth in the rude Kentucky cabin on February 12, 1809 to Tom Lincoln and the former Nancy Hanks; of Nancy's death in 1818; of Tom's remarriage to Sarah Bush; of Abe's rough, rural boyhood in Kentucky, Indiana, and, finally, Illinois. We can all see him full-grown, a lean six feet, four inches, strong with dark, deep-set eyes, and gaunt, sunken cheeks; and most of us know that he came to New Salem, as he put it, "no more than a floating piece of driftwood" in 1831.

More pertinent to our purposes here are his personal relationships, particularly those with women. If we start with the young boy, there was considerable tenderness between the boy and Nancy and much less between the boy and Tom. But it was his stepmother, Sarah, who gave him the love and emotional stability which all souls need in youth. Sandburg describes her as "a strong, large-boned, rosy woman with a kindly face and eyes, a steady voice, steady ways. From the first she was warm and friendly for Abe's hands to touch."

Of Lincoln's love affair with Ann Rutledge, much less is known. Sandburg is very cautious in describing their relationship. "It was certain that Ann Rutledge and Lincoln knew each other and he took an interest in her...probably they formed some mutual attachment...possibly they loved each other." But he also quotes Ann's cousin McGrady as saying that "Lincoln took Ann's death very hard," and thirty years afterward, Herndon and some New Salem villagers wrote of "what a deep flaming of lyric love there had been between Abe and Ann."

For the most part, Abe was uncomfortable and self-conscious around women. Sarah Bush Lincoln wrote that "he liked people in general, children and animals, but was not very fond of girls." New Salem co-worker A. Y. Ellis was more explicit. "He always disliked to wait on the ladies. He preferred trading with men and boys...He was a very shy man of ladies...I thought it was on account of his awkward appearance and his wearing apparel."

Richard Current tells an interesting story about Lincoln and women. It occurred in Springfield not long before the arrival of Mary Todd. In need of female company, Abe asked his friend Joshua Speed if there were any accommodating ladies in town. Speed sent him to a prostitute, and upon getting into bed with her, Abe asked how much the evening would cost. She replied, "Five dollars." "I only have three," answered the embarrassed Lincoln, "and I won't do this on credit." So he rose, dressed, and left the room, his mission unaccomplished, with the prostitute calling after him, "Mr. Lincoln, you are the most contentious man I ever saw!"

Abe's relationship with Mary Todd was always a stormy one. Their courtship was a perfect example. When Mary's affair with Douglas drove him to stand her up on New Year's Day of 1841, Lincoln became mentally distraught. Speed and some other friends searched for him all night, and when they found him the next morning, he was nearly suicidal. They removed his razor and knife from him, and counseled him to get away from Springfield for awhile. It was Speed who took him back to Kentucky and tended to him until he was emotionally recovered. For the next year, Abe wrestled with himself over Mary, finally yielding to a sense of destiny about her. He believed that "God," or "Fate," or "Necessity" was a great instrument in his life, and he maintained that belief to the end. Not long before his murder, he confided as President to Congressman Isaac Arnold, "I have all my life been a fatalist. What is to be, will be...As Hamlet says, 'There is a divinity that shapes our ends, rough-hew them how we will'."

Joshua Speed. Lincoln's relationship with Speed did not begin in New Salem, as our play suggests, but in Springfield in 1837. Speed, indeed, came to Illinois from Kentucky just as Abe did, but the two had not migrated together. Speed had come to open up a store, and it was into that store that Abe walked in 1837 to buy a bed. Speed quoted him a price of $17, and lacking that amount, Lincoln asked if he might buy the bed on credit. "I think I can suggest a plan by which you will be able to attain your end without incurring any debt," Speed answered. "I have a very large room and a very large double bed in it which you are perfectly welcome to share with me if you choose." Lincoln accepted the offer and found not only a roommate but a lifelong friend.

After Lincoln's mental recuperation in 1841 at the Speed farm near Louisville, Kentucky, Joshua sold the Springfield store and began managing his family's business in Farmington. Lincoln returned to Illinois, and the two corresponded throughout 1842. When Speed fell in love with and subsequently married a Kentucky girl named Fanny Henning, Lincoln wrote asking if the institution of marriage was a sound one. "Are you now in feeling as well as judgment, glad you are married as you are?" Speed answered in the affirmative and told his friend that he should either do the same with Mary Todd or forget her forever. Apparently, Lincoln took the advice.

The correspondence between the two men lasted all of Lincoln's life. They wrote about women, politics, and, increasingly, about the issue of slavery which was dividing the nation. A letter from Speed to Lincoln dated 1855 reveals the growing philosophical gap between the two friends. While not condoning slavery in the abstract, Speed wrote that he "would rather see the Union dissolve than yield his legal right to own a slave." Again, in 1856, he wrote to Lincoln. "So fixed is public sentiment in this state against...allowing Negroes to be emancipated and remain among us, that you had as well attack the freedom of worship in the North, or the right of a parent to teach his child to read." And Lincoln responded with his now famous quote on slavery. "As a nation, we began by declaring that 'all men are created equal'...We now practically read it 'all men are created equal except Negroes'."

Political differences, however, never separated Speed from his friend. Even after Lincoln's election to the Presidency, Speed went to Washington to visit Abe at the White House. He commented later that Lincoln was "toilworn and worried" over the impending outbreak of war. What kind of farewell they took of each other, whether or not they might have laughed over the old days in Springfield, we shall never know.

Stephen Douglas. That Douglas was Lincoln's rival in both love and politics is certainly true. That he was a lifelong expansionist and tolerant, if not approving, of slavery is equally true. But in the end, Douglas proved himself a devoted statesman, serving to his death the President he had so often opposed.

Stephen Douglas was born on April 13, 1813 in Brandon, Vermont but left New England to become a teacher in Jacksonville, Illinois at the age of twenty. His eloquence and intelligence led him quickly to the law and to politics. He soon found himself in Vandalia representing Morgan County and shortly thereafter was appointed State's Attorney for the First Judicial Circuit and Judge of the Illinois Supreme Court.

Always a loyal Democrat, Douglas was elected to the House of Representatives in 1843 where he earned the nickname "The Little Giant." His chubby five-foot, four-inch frame might not have won any beauty contests, but his powers of oration soon catapulted him to the Senate where he remained until his death. He ran unsuccessfully for the Democratic Presidential nomination in both 1852 and 1856, and entered into the famous series of debates with Lincoln in 1858 when Lincoln challenged him for the Illinois Senate seat. Although Lincoln beat him in the popular election, Douglas retained his office by vote of the Illinois State Legislature and returned to Washington to gear up for the 1860 Presidential Campaign.

By then the Democratic Party had been split in two on the slavery issue. The northern wing, headed by Douglas, supported the right of new states and territories to decide themselves if they wished to be slave or free land. "It all comes down to the principle of dollars and cents," Douglas argued. "The decision should be with the white people of the affected area." As between the white man and the Negro, Douglas declared he would always favor the white man. As between the Negro and a crocodile, he would favor the Negro. Not even this position, however, could satisfy the party's southern wing who found their own champion in Breckinridge of Kentucky.

Douglas was given the Presidential nomination of the northern Democrats. He came in second to Lincoln out of a field of four candidates, garnering only twelve electoral college votes. On hearing of Lincoln's victory, he said, "Mr. Lincoln is the next President. We must try to save the Union." From that moment until his death on June 3, 1861, he gave himself tirelessly to the service of his rival, traveling endless hours to southern, western, and border states, pleading for the nation to avoid a Civil War. "Fiercely unmindful of the toll on his spent body," as Benjamin Thomas puts it, Douglas campaigned unsuccessfully for the preservation of the Union until he succumbed to exhaustion at his home in Chicago.

An item in the Cincinnati Commercial, printed shortly before Douglas's death, seemed to capture for many the spirit of The Little Giant. Having lost the Presidency to Lincoln, Douglas found himself seated near his old nemesis on the podium at which Lincoln was to give his inaugural address. When Lincoln got up to speak, he discovered that he had no place for his hat and cane. Seeing the problem, it was Douglas who rose and without a word took the articles to hold for the new President on whose shoulders now rested the fate of the nation.

About the play. *The Prairie Man* was researched and written between 1985 and 1989. It is decidedly a work of fiction, drawing freely on historical fact and real characters, but bending them to the needs of the stage and the structure of story theatre.

If there was any single thing which inspired the play, it was the insistence of Lincoln's law partner, William Herndon, that Ann Rutledge was the inspiration for Lincoln's achievements, not just during the brief period she and Abe shared their love, but for all the years after her death. The dead do speak to us, if not in actuality then in our memories of them and in the works they leave behind. Beethoven talks through his symphonies, Dickens through his books, and it seems to be that Ann spoke to Abe through the love she left him and her legacy to him of self-worth and the willingness to try to rise to his true level of ability.

Many of the scenes in *The Prairie Man* actually happened. Most of the Lincoln-Douglas debate scene actually occurred. Many of Lincoln's humorous anecdotes are reportedly true. Here and there, even lines of dialogue such as Lincoln's phrase to Ann, "I don't wish to be more presuming than what becomes me," were really uttered. The flow of political events in the play happened in pretty much the order depicted.

One does not write a work like *The Prairie Man* in a vacuum, and I am enormously indebted to authors like Carl Sandburg, Benjamin Thomas, Richard Current, Paul Angle, and Stefan Lorrant for providing the raw material for much of the play.

The Prairie Man was first produced in the summer of 1990 at the Helen Foley Theatre in Binghamton, N. Y. The set design by Lawrence Kassan enabled us to change locations using rear-screen projection and simulate crowds through the use of back-lit panels at the extremes of stage left and right. You can see some of these effects in the photos of this edition. The result of Mr. Kassan's design was that we could play the work using only the characters of Ann, Abe, Douglas, Mary, and Speed, who also doubled as Jessie Fell, the Speaker of the Illinois Legislature.

Using Speed to go in and out of character and to effect all the changes of scenery as he spoke his narration allowed us to achieve a tremendous intimacy in our performances. By directing Speed to enter and exit through the audience as well as the stage, we bound the audience even more tightly to the action.

In January of 1991, a second production was mounted at the Foley Theatre with the same cast. Again, we opted for the same set and the same staging, this time adding pre-recorded nineteenth century string quartet music to set the mood. Given a theatre capable of it, I think I would direct it again in the same way.

Steven Porter
January 1992

x

The Prairie Man

ACT I

SCENE 1

(The stage is open, and a few sparse pieces suggest the rough interior of a Midwestern country store early in the 19th century. To either side of center are bleacher sections each capable of seating a dozen or so people. From time to time they may be illuminated and decorated to suggest a location or event. Now they are plain and dark.

JOSHUA SPEED enters hauling an oaken barrel of considerable weight. He is wearing boots and a heavy coat. He sets the barrel down and as he speaks removes his coat, hangs it up, and generally makes himself more comfortable.)

SPEED: *(to the audience)* 'Mornin'. I reckon where you are you can get good and warm of a January mornin'. Not here. Not in New Salem. 'Course you folks got all them gadgets can cook your food and cozy your blankets. We ain't got none of that yet. Maybe eighty, ninety years, but not now. Now it's eighteen hundred and thirty two in the year of our good Lord, and he can sure make a January smart. Yessir! 'Course if we had a railway spur down from Chicago, we wouldn't be haulin' no nails by wagon through that there snow outside, let me tell you. It'd be a damn sight easier—pardon the language, ladies—than sloggin' through the woods from Springfield. But some people just can't see it. They don't want no railroad, no outsiders, no comforts from the big city. Nothing. They're gonna slog it out every winter, and you mind me, they're gonna freeze doing it, and they'll love it! They'll turn to you with the ice drippin' off their noses and their lungs full of the dropsy and they'll say they don't want it no other way. Sometimes the prairie people is just touched. Well...we'll get back to that later. I gotta introduce myself. Speed is what they call me. My mother back in Kentucky was partial to the Bible, and they tell me when I was just born she was readin' that part where they was fighting over Jericho, so she called me Joshua. Joshua Speed. Never loved it, but it's all I got. And now you ask what's Joshua Speed doing in New Salem, Illinois sloggin' through a January snow storm haulin' nails in the year of our Lord eighteen hundred and thirty-two? Hmm!! I'm doin' it for my friend...who's out there by the wagons, who don't like the railroads, who prefers to travel by the river, and who's gonna get me good and buried by the time he's done! *(calling outside)* Hey, Abraham! You comin' in here this winter or you gonna build yourself a igloo out there! *(to the audience)* The man is a lunatic for hard work! If there's a two-foot wall and a three-foot wall to climb, he's gonna take the three-foot wall. And I mean every time. Which is fine if he's climbin' by himself. What wall a man takes ain't no one's business but his own. Except if you're climbin' with him. Then it's your knees get scraped up...Ah, but he's my friend, too, I guess. Anyways, we knowed each other from way back in Kentucky, and we stuck it through a lot of winters, not that we're all that old. But it's gotta be ten or twelve since Abe was a boy at least. *(calling again to the outside)* Hey, them horses put away yet? *(to the audience)* Now you mind when he comes in here you don't take to none of that riverboat stuff. The railroad is the way of the future. That is plain and everybody knows it no matter what he says...could talk a rabbit right outta the burrow, that man. I tell you, yessir!

(ABRAHAM LINCOLN enters. He is twenty-two, tall and lean. Like SPEED he wears boots and a coat, removing them during the dialogue. If there is a stove with coffee, the two men can drink as they talk.)

LINCOLN: Lord, but it's a cold day for haulin' nails through the woods.

SPEED: Now how'd I'd know you was gonna bring up that river?

LINCOLN: What river, Joshua? I was talkin' about the woods.

SPEED: The river that runs along the woods. I know your mind!

LINCOLN: Seems I didn't say anything at all. But if you wanna unburden your soul about our sweet river, I'd be pleased to listen to you.

SPEED: You know the railway's gotta come, Abe.

LINCOLN: *(working on his boots)* I'm still listening.

SPEED: It's the future, certain and true. People's movin' west. Chicago gotta have ten, maybe fifteen thousand by now.

LINCOLN: I expect even more than that.

SPEED: Well there, you see? And it's just natural some of them are gonna wanna trickle on down toward Springfield.

LINCOLN: What about those who wanna trickle on up from St. Louis? Can't take a Chicago railroad train from Missouri.

SPEED: St. Louis! Overcooked food, loose women, and watered-down liquor! Who wants anything in St. Louis?

LINCOLN: I think there might be one or two residents could take exception to that.

SPEED: You just filled up with the place 'cause old man Offutt sent you down there on a flatboat!

(The door opens and ANN RUTLEDGE enters. She is eighteen years old, delicate and beautiful. LINCOLN rises in polite greeting, boots in hand.)

LINCOLN: Mornin', Miss Rutledge.

ANN: Please, don't trouble, Mr. Lincoln. I just came in for some of those fancy canned goods you got. Mornin', Mr. Speed.

SPEED: Mornin', Miss Rutledge.

ANN: *(as she shops)* Certainly is a cold mornin' this mornin'.

SPEED: Particularly if you got a mind to take a flatboat down the river!

ANN: The river! Why it's nearly frozen full over!

LINCOLN: Don't mind him, Miss Rutledge. We were only havin' a conversation.

ANN: Well don't let me interrupt, Mr. Lincoln. I gotta tend to these goods anyway. *(She resumes shopping.)*

SPEED: You see there? The girl says the river is froze full over! Now how you gonna get a boat up that river in winter?

LINCOLN: *(putting his boots back on)* Which river, Josh? The Sangamon, the Illinois, or the Mississippi?

SPEED: What's the difference? They're all froze. Same weather here in New Salem as they got in Beardstown and St. Louis!

LINCOLN: But the Illinois and Mississippi's got current and depth. Take a lot more winter than we got here to freeze them over.

SPEED: Oh, fine! So the Illinois and Mississippi stays open while the Sangamon freezes! And we haul our goods in the dead of January all the way from Beardstown!

LINCOLN: Well, maybe not...

SPEED: What do you mean, maybe not? They ain't gonna haul themselves! Look at what old man Offutt's doing in Beardstown right now. Why this is his own store, and he can't get them supplies he fetched from St. Louis up the Sangamon. Probably gonna have to wait for the thaw just to get himself up here.

LINCOLN: I expect it's more the liquor in Beardstown than the weather that's keepin' him.

SPEED: Smart man!

ANN: *(finishing)* I think that's the lot, Mr. Lincoln.

SPEED: *(as LINCOLN checks her goods)* Now with a railway spur, there'd be no river, no layin' up in Beardstown. Why they got a plow on them engines can clear a track full of snow from here to Chicago faster 'n we can haul them nails to Miss Rutledge's—assumin' you got a mind to take 'em, ma'am.

ANN: The canned goods will be quite enough, Mr. Speed.

LINCOLN: That comes to eighty-six cents, Miss Rutledge.

ANN: *(as she pays)* You know, if you gentlemen really want to discuss this, why don't you come to the house Saturday night? Father's got the meeting of the Debating Society. I think they'd be most interested in hearing you.

LINCOLN: *(placing the food in a basket)* Let me help you with these, Miss Rutledge.

ANN: Thank you, Mr. Lincoln. I can manage.

SPEED: You say Saturday?

ANN: *(as LINCOLN holds the door for her)* Yes, Mr. Speed. We'd be pleased to see you there. *(to LINCOLN)* Both of you.

LINCOLN: Good day, Miss Rutledge. *(She exits as the two men resume their former posture.)*

SPEED: You know, that ain't a bad idea, Abe. Saturday at the Rutledges'.

LINCOLN: *(rising)* You think maybe she could use some help with the wagon? *(He puts his coat on and exits after her.)*

(The lighting dims on center stage. SPEED moves into a spot and addresses the audience.)

SPEED: James Rutledge founded New Salem, him and John Camron. He come up from South Carolina. Lived in Georgia, Tennessee, and— bless his heart—Kentucky before he put his roots into Illinois. Ann's his third. He's got nine, and I reckon a pretty understanding wife.

Anyways, the Debatin' Society hereabouts is more than Saturday night hollerin'. More like what you'd call a town meetin'. After the jawin' and scratchin' is over, folks kind of take a vote. It ain't bindin', mind you, in a legal sort of way, but prairie people ain't ones to go changin' after they come out public for a thing. I guess they must be ready for us now.

(He walks from the spot to center stage which comes up decorated simply to suggest the Rutledge House. The bleacher sections, now also illuminated, are filled with the citizens of New Salem who attentively listen to SPEED as he talks. LINCOLN stands near the section in which ANN is seated. As SPEED makes his way into the set, we are in Scene 2.)

SCENE 2

SPEED: So even though I ain't what you call a natural Illinois bred boy, I reckon Kentucky ain't the other end of the world neither, folks there bein' about the same as folks here, and I tell you they'd love to be hitched up to the Chicago line. Yessir! Can you imagine? Calicos right from the mill, and maybe some of that fancy New York lace for the ladies! And how about not havin' to wait five weeks for your tea and barreled pork? Why the railroad is a vein carryin' the life blood of our country, and I say it'd be almost ungodly to turn our backs on it.

(The bleachers applaud. SPEED stands off to one side while LINCOLN moves slowly to the center of the set. He is awkward and nervous at first but gains in power throughout his speech.)

LINCOLN: I...I don't know much about...I mean...ungodly...that's mighty strong language...seems it's right difficult at times to know what's ungodly and...and what's not. I remember back in Indiana when I was growin' up we had this preacher. Godly as you'd ever want standin' up there sayin' his sermon. Till once a little blue lizard run right up his pants leg...well, there he was, Bible in one hand, scratchin' this and scratchin' that with the other so's everyone thought he was a blasphemer. They run him right out of the church for bein' ungodly, and all the poor fella did was protect himself like any natural man...

(The bleachers react with laughter. LINCOLN waits, then continues.)

Now I am no enemy of the railroad. I agree with Mr. Speed that it is a vein to the very heart of our land. But if it be the vein, then our rivers are surely the arteries. And the question is not which we eliminate but which is preferable for our community at this time. What do we gain with a railroad? Goods from Chicago? Yes. Certainly, and that would be a convenience. But not for New Salem. No railway spur is goin' to come to New Salem before it goes to Springfield first. We'll be payin' a wagonload of our dollars and end up haulin' goods just like we do now. We'll have more goods, but we'll be doin' a lot more haulin' and payin' a lot more for the privilege.

(The bleachers react as LINCOLN begins to win them over.)

On the other hand, we could dredge the Sangamon and make it fit for riverboat travel summer and winter. Then consider what we got. Goods up the Mississippi from New Orleans and St. Louis. Riverboats up the Illinois to Beardstown and then across the Sangamon right to our door and right on into Springfield dock. For half what it'd cost us to build a rail spur, we'd have the same calicos and laces, barreled pork and tea, and a whole lot more than that. Why a riverboat can bring people and traveling shows and new ideas you just can't get off a freight train.

(Again the bleachers react.)

Now I can see a time for the railroad. Let us grow a bit and we'll have lines to Vandalia and Peoria and Springfield and New Salem, too. But now's a time for the river. A good dredgin' and a new dock, a coat of shiny white paint straight from Offutt's to the Springfield wharf, and then let that old paddlewheel come. And I promise you, she will carry no blue lizards in her cargo hold.

(The bleachers applaud enthusiastically. ANN rises.)

ANN: Father and I would be pleased if you'd all adjourn to the parlour where you can take your refreshment and vote your mind.

(The bleachers empty slowly and fade to black. SPEED exits with the others while LINCOLN and ANN linger behind.)

LINCOLN: I wonder if they took to my view of things.

ANN: You spoke elegantly, Mr. Lincoln. I shouldn't wonder at all. Why a man who speaks as you do...well, I shouldn't wonder at all.

LINCOLN: It's nothin' so far out of the ordinary, Miss Rutledge. Nothin' many a man here mightn't do...and a whole lot less than some with real educatin'.

ANN: You've had no schoolin' at all, Mr Lincoln?

LINCOLN: Some when I was younger...in Indiana...and some from Mentor Greene right here in New Salem.

ANN: Mentor Greene? You mean at his home?

LINCOLN: Sometimes there. Sometimes at Offutt's when he comes in for his tobacco. Mostly at his fireside, I guess.

ANN: He has a daughter, doesn't he?

LINCOLN: Why...why yes...I don't much see her around, though.

ANN: Well, with Mentor Greene on the job, Mr. Lincoln, there's no tellin' how elegant you might become.

(She takes his arm and escorts him toward the parlour. The set fades. SPEED appears in a spot.)

SPEED: Beat me deader'n a rail. When the whole town got done votin' it was two hundred seventy-seven for Abe outta three hundred cast. And then he organizes a whole river committee. Some folks clearin' brush, some puttin' up bank levees. Now the heavy dredgin' went to Abe and the Armstrong boys from Clary's Grove. Worked all that winter and most of the spring gettin' ready for the Talisman. She wasn't the biggest boat in the territory, but she was a cargo steamer right and true. Small, light draft, and able to take any water clear to Cincinnati. She come down the Ohio to Cairo, then north up the Mississippi to St. Louis where she picked up her merchandise for the folks in Sangamon County. Then onto the Illinois for Beardstown and east again along Abe's new-dredged stream, right into Springfield wharf. It was sure a sight for the people who stood along the banks wavin' 'n cheerin' till the Talisman would disappear around the next bend, and when she finally come into harbor, folks was ready to bust. They took over the court house and threw themselves a party lasted right through the night and on into the next day. And there was Abe in the center of it. A hero, kind of, on account of its all bein' his idea. If there was ever a moment to say the prairie folks seen the greatness of the man for the first time, it was that night in Springfield in 1832 when the Talisman come to dock.

(SPEED moves from the spot to center stage which now appears festooned as the Springfield Court House. The party is in full swing with couples dancing in folk style. ANN and LINCOLN are unobtrusive participants. We are now in Scene 3.)

SCENE 3

(When the revelry is over SPEED ascends to a place of prominence and addresses the crowd.)

SPEED: Quiet down now, folks...quiet down and gather round. That's it, Mr. Rutledge...Mr. Armstrong...move in here. *(The crowd quiets.)* I guess there ain't one of you doesn't know what this day means to our part of Illinois, or who's the man most responsible for it. *(The crowd cheers, and we can clearly make out the name Lincoln on more than one person's lips.)* Quiet down now...Abe, I've been asked as your friend to speak for the political committee of New Salem. Elections comin' up, and a lot of hard decisions gonna have to be made in Vandalia next year. No doubt about the need for good men to represent our interests. What with all you done to bring our riverboat here, we reckon there ain't no one we'd like speakin' for us more than you. *(The crowd cheers. SPEED quiets them again.)* What do you say, Abe? Will you run for the Assembly and represent the folks of New Salem?

(Eyes turn to LINCOLN. The crowd freezes. The lights dim. A spot picks him up as he walks from center stage to one side. It is night now. Everything around him is black and still. Slowly, the railing of the Talisman's deck becomes visible, shimmering as the moon plays off the waters of the Sangamon River. LINCOLN stares into the night. After a moment, ANN enters. It is Scene 4.)

SCENE 4

ANN: It isn't the best form to leave your constituents without an answer, Mr. Assemblyman.

LINCOLN: Good evenin', Ann.

ANN: *(after a pause)* I love the river when it's like this. Cool and quiet.

LINCOLN: There's gonna be Indian trouble, Ann. Soon. Governor Reynolds has asked for volunteers.

ANN: And you're goin', aren't you, Abe?

LINCOLN: He wants four hundred from Sangamon County alone.

ANN: Why so many? We've never had that much to do with the Indians.

LINCOLN: It's Black Hawk, the way I heard it.

ANN: But didn't he sign a treaty with President Jackson?

LINCOLN: Indians don't sign away their lands any more than black folks sign away their freedom. President Jackson knows that well enough.

ANN: Seems to me you're taking up with Black Hawk's side of things.

LINCOLN: Black Hawk's an old man, Ann. He's almost seventy and he's seen his people pushed out of land they've hunted nearly five hundred years. He's scared. He's got his back to the wall, like a cornered bear. And that makes him dangerous.

ANN: So you are goin' to fight him.

LINCOLN: It's not an easy world, Miss Rutledge. There are things in this land—like the Indians and slavery—run deep and wrong...only...

ANN: Only what, Abe?

LINCOLN: Only fightin's not the way. I wish it could be that every man might receive at least a moderate education...to read the histories of his own and other peoples and come to appreciate the value of freedom...history and the Scriptures...

ANN: Abe, why not run for the Assembly?

LINCOLN: I told you, I'm answerin' the Governor's call.

ANN: The election's not until August. You'll be back in time to campaign.

LINCOLN: I don't wish to be more presumin' than what becomes me.

ANN: I think the State Assembly becomes you just fine, Mr. Lincoln.

(The lights fade and pick up SPEED in a spot once again.)

SPEED: Abe served eighty days in the Black Hawk War, risin' to the rank of Captain. He was mustered out on July nineteenth, eighteen hundred and thirty-two and for his troubles received the sum of ninety-five dollars from the United States Army. For the first time in his life, he saw the death of men close up, and he profoundly resolved that he should never see it again. It was less than three weeks to the state election. He campaigned across the county on a platform favorin' equal taxation, education, and an end to the Indian conflict. The results come down from Springfield, evenin' of August sixth.

(The lights fade on SPEED and come up on Offutt's store. LINCOLN enters opening a letter. He reads it, places it down on the counter, moves to one of the shelves, and starts to arrange a stack of dry goods. ANN enters behind him, studying him with care. She puts her basket on the

counter, picks up the letter and reads it to herself. When she is done, she puts it down slowly and continues toward him.)

ANN: At least you got ninety percent of New Salem.

LINCOLN: *(turning)* Good evening, Ann.

ANN: Abe, I am sorry.

LINCOLN: Well, eighth out of thirteen runnin' isn't the end of the world.

ANN: What will you do now?

LINCOLN: I don't know. Buy the store, maybe. I think Offutt's goin' to sell, and I'd like to remain among the folks who have treated me so kindly.

ANN: Abe, I'm not the one to tell you what to do...especially after the way I encouraged you for the Assembly...

LINCOLN: Seems unfair to blame yourself for how folks voted.

ANN: And it seems folks never had a chance to hear you, Abe. Not really hear you. Not like I hear you.

LINCOLN: Maybe they heard all they cared to.

ANN: No, Abe. You were right about the Black Hawk War. Why, while you were away everyone in town come to see things just like you said.

LINCOLN: But that's just it, Ann. New Salem's hardly the whole county. I just spoke for the town.

ANN: So speak for the county, Mr. Lincoln. There must be many a way to do it.

LINCOLN: Mentor Greene thinks I ought to study for Postmaster and Surveyor—

ANN: Well there you are, then.

LINCOLN: I don't even have the books. There's Flint's "Treatise on Geometry" and the "Theory of Surveyin'" and Gibbon's "Decline and Fall..."

ANN: Why Father's got the "Decline and Fall," and I'm sure whatever else you need Mentor Greene can get for you.

LINCOLN: And what about the law books? I've got to know the law as well.

ANN: Mr. Stuart's Father's lawyer. He's got a whole library in Springfield. It's only eighteen miles, Abe...and I'd be pleased to help you study.

LINCOLN: Would you, Miss Rutledge...

(The lights fade on Scene 4 and pick up SPEED in a spot off to one side.)

SCENE 5

SPEED: Wasn't long after the election of thirty-two James Rutledge sold a part of his farm to John McNeil. Strange man, McNeil. Comes out to the prairie from New York, buys a heap of land, then heads right back East. Some folks say there was more than land to the Rutledge deal, that maybe Ann figured in it. Maybe a promise of marriage along with the Illinois soil so's the land could be sold and still remain in the Rutledge bloodline. Maybe. But McNeil sure never claimed her, pretty as she was. If anything, with him a way back in New York tendin' to whatever mysterious business he was about, it was Abe got most of her time. Wasn't hardly a day you'd ride past the big oak outside of town that you wouldn't see the two of them propped up against it, him readin' out loud or talkin' to her somethin' fierce about this thing or that. *(He begins to drift offstage.)* Got so's she spent more time with him than I did. And here I was, all the way up from Kentucky with the man...

(SPEED exits. The lights come up on a wooded knoll near New Salem. An oak branch gives its shelter to the ground and although there is not much scenery, the place has a feeling of warmth. During the scene the branch changes to reflect the passage of time—budding in the Spring, brown-leafed in the Fall, full-leafed in the Summer. At rise, ANN is on a blanket beneath the bough. LINCOLN stands astride the knoll, book in hand. It is the Spring of 1833.)

LINCOLN: "And if it be that the recipient is no longer living, then the mail directed to him—or her— shall be returned by the Postmaster unopened with the appropriate explanation."

ANN: Sounds clear enough.

LINCOLN: Except it doesn't say who's to pay the postage on the return.

ANN: You're always looking at the dark side, Abe. They're not going to ask you who's to pay a dead man's postage. *(She takes the book.)*

LINCOLN: God only knows what they're goin' to ask, and I hope it isn't somethin' about the new rates. Six cents a sheet for the first thirty miles, and ten cents for the first eighty; two sheets for twelve cents; three for eighteen cents; two bits for four hundred miles...

ANN: Seems you remember it just fine. Now how much would it be to send a three-sheet letter from Springfield to Boston?

LINCOLN: Seventy-five cents, I reckon.

ANN: Why that's absolutely correct, Mr. Lincoln!

(Speed reappears in a spot as the lights fade on LINCOLN and ANN.)

SPEED: On May seventh, eighteen thirty-three, Abe was appointed Postal Director of New Salem, his pay runnin' about fifty dollars a year in commission on receipts. The mail come in twice a week by rider or stagecoach. Letters, mostly, folded and wax sealed, there bein' no envelopes invented yet. Back then, it was the receiver who paid the postage, not the sender like you folks do today. A letter or package come in, and Abe would have to figure its weight, or how many sheets it had, and how far it'd come, and then he'd compute the amount due and collect it from the receivin' party. Most Postmasters had fixed hours. Not Abe. He'd leave the store open so's anyone could fetch his own mail, and more often than not he'd trust 'em for the money due. Maybe it was just the nature of prairie folk, but they always paid. Then again, maybe it was the way they held Abe.

(SPEED exits. The lights come up on the wooded knoll. The bough shows us that it is now Fall. ANN, appropriately dressed, stands quizzing a reclining LINCOLN on the mathematics of surveying.)

ANN: "...two hundred yards from the house to the creek, and six hundred feet to the county road. What is his total acreage, and at the current rates what does he owe for the land?"

LINCOLN: You say two hundred yards from the house?

ANN: To the creek. Yes. And six hundred feet to the road.

LINCOLN: That's a clean ninety degrees on his North side, so we've got a right triangle on our hands. *(He rises and moves toward her.)* That table of logarithms in there?

ANN: *(flipping to the rear of the book)* Yes sir. Right here.

LINCOLN: *(moving close to her as she holds the book for him)* Let's see. Two point five five. Times the forty acres we had...comes to one hundred and two.

ANN: *(staying close to him)* Yes, that's right.

LINCOLN: And at two dollars per, he owes two hundred four dollars on the land. That's the answer. Two hundred four dollars.

ANN: *(hugging his arm)* Yes, it is indeed, Mr. Lincoln...now try this one...

(The lights fade on the knoll and come up again on SPEED.)

SPEED: *(reading from a legal-looking document)* "The clerk of Sangamon County Surveyor's Office deputes to Mr. Abraham Lincoln that portion of work within his part of the county. Fees fixed by this office not to exceed two dollars fifty cents for establishing one quarter section of land; two dollars for the half-quarter; and no more than thirty-seven and one half cents for the town lot." Well, he wasn't goin' to get rich at those rates, but it was technical work of a very responsible nature. Folks depended on him for the legal titles to their farms, and the county depended on him for the rates of taxation. By the Summer of eighteen thirty-four, he had worked most of his section of the countryside, and there was hardly a person between New Salem and Springfield didn't know and respect him.

(SPEED exits. LINCOLN and ANN appear seated together at the oak, a book now shared on both their laps. It is Spring, 1834.)

LINCOLN: "...to the aggrieved party, judgment shall be rendered within sixty days not to exceed one half the estate."

ANN: And in the case of accident?

LINCOLN: The same time but no more than one third.

ANN: And in Kentucky?

LINCOLN: One third but ninety days to judgment.

ANN: *(closing the book and rising)* That's all of it. You know it dead cold.

LINCOLN: And you think I could make another run for Assembly?

ANN: *(turning)* You'll win, Abe. And with another year or two you'll pass the Bar.

LINCOLN: *(rising to her)* And what will you be doin' while I'm tendin' to the legislature away off in Vandalia, Miss Rutledge.

ANN: I've got the farm...and Father's talked of sending me to school...

LINCOLN: Ann, I came to New Salem not much more than a floatin' piece of driftwood...

ANN: *(placing her fingers to his lips)* You don't have to say anything, Abe.

(They freeze in position as the lights fade on Scene 5.)

SCENE 6

(SPEED appears in a spot off to one side. Behind in dim lighting stage center we see the State Assembly chamber in Vandalia. The bleachers have become the seats of the legislature while the center of the set contains a speaker's platform. As SPEED talks, the chamber fills with delegates. They are all men.)

SPEED: It was seventy-five miles from New Salem to the state capitol in Vandalia. Abe covered it in two days by stage, arrivin' the last week of November, eighteen thirty-four. Already the town was festooned for the new session, liquor and tobacco, good food and cheap boardin' house rooms aboundin'. He was one of three dozen freshman legislators, and a loyal member of the Whigs. As such, there wasn't much love lost between him and the Democrats who supported President Andy Jackson down in Washington. My Lord, but Abe had never seen so much of the opposition party, most of New Salem bein' Whig like him. There was not only the varmints in the legislature to contend with, but all manner of folk lobbyin' for this and that in every tavern, every hotel, every law office in the town. And there was one he come to know in particular that first year. Little dwarf of a fella. Lawyer from the First Circuit recently appointed to the position of State's Attorney.

(The lights fade on SPEED and come up stage center. We see the SPEAKER of the Assembly at his podium with the legislature on the bleachers to either side.)

SPEAKER: The Chair recognizes Stephen Douglas.

(DOUGLAS rises from his seat on the bleachers and assumes the podium.)

DOUGLAS: In the initial matter of the State Surveyor for the Springfield region, it has come to my attention that the incumbent, Mr. Coleman Smoot, has passed away. I would nominate to this body Mr. Samuel McHatton as his replacement.

SPEAKER: Seconds?

VOICE FROM THE CROWD: I second.

SPEAKER: In favor?

LEGISLATURE: Aye.

SPEAKER: Opposed?

LINCOLN: *(standing)* No.

SPEAKER: The "ayes" have it. Mr. McHatton will be notified by Post at once.

DOUGLAS: In the second matter of legislative procedure, I am not quite sure what the gentleman from Sangamon County is proposing. Does he wish to allow us no amendments on our bills, or are we to continue with the present policy of unlimited amendment privileges?

LINCOLN: *(rising)* Neither case, Mr. Speaker.

DOUGLAS: Well, there being no prohibition on the one hand and no limitation on the other, I move the matter be tabled for some future consideration.

SPEAKER: Seconds?

VOICE: I second.

SPEAKER: In favor?

LEGISLATURE: Aye.

SPEAKER: Opposed?

LINCOLN: *(standing)* No.

SPEAKER: The "ayes" have it. The motion is carried.

(The members of the Legislature freeze as the lights fade on the Assembly chamber. A spot picks up SPEED off to one side.)

SPEED: Stephen Arnold Douglas was a Democrat sure enough. Contrary. Cantankerous. Just full of the law and the power of government. He come to Vandalia as a teacher. Books and city ways were no strangers to him like they was to Abe. But Abe was a prairie man. He knew other things. Like for instance he knew what made the winter wheat to growin' and how to trap the crafty prairie fox...

(The light dims on SPEED and comes up again stage center where the Legislature resumes its action. LINCOLN rises holding a letter in his hand.)

SPEAKER: The chair recognizes Mr. Lincoln of New Salem.

LINCOLN: Thank you, Mr. Speaker. *(holding the letter and walking to the podium)* In the initial matter of the appointment of a successor to Mr. Smoot of Springfield, I wish to announce to the gentlemen that the deceased has rallied and appears ready to resume his duties. *(The chamber reacts.)* I took the liberty of writin' home to Dr. John Allen of New Salem and he tells me he's been most successful in reversin' Mr. Smoot's condition. I therefore move that as long as the man persists in not dyin' we vacate Mr. McHatton's appointment. *(There is laughter from the chamber.)* Not wishin', of course, to call any adversity on Mr. Douglas, I would also move that in the future event of Mr. Smoot's demise, Mr. Douglas's nominee be given the job. *(laughter again)*

VOICE: I second!

SPEAKER: So moved. In favor?

LEGISLATURE: Aye!

SPEAKER: I take it there is no opposition. Motion is approved.

LINCOLN: Thank you, Mr. Speaker. Now to the matter of procedure. I think we may all agree that on one or two occasions, we have engaged in the practice of amendin' our bills right into an early grave. *(laughter from the legislators)* I think even Mr. Douglas has witnessed the use of the amendment process to such ends. *(laughter)* Now I recall he said something about prohibition on the one hand and unlimited use on the other, and that brings to mind the case of Mentor Greene and the New Salem Church. Seems that when Mentor Greene joined the temperance movement, the church elders—bein' good drinkin' men—saw fit to suspend him. But so as not to seem unreasonable, when Mr. Camron of Salt Creek appeared at Sunday worship somewhat liquored up, they suspended him too. Which puzzled Mentor Greene greatly, and in an effort to establish some firm policy caused him to approach the elders with a bottle of good Illinois spirits in his hands. "I have seen you," he called out wavin' the bottle on high, "suspend one member for drinkin' too much and another member for not drinkin' at all. And what I wish to know from you gentlemen is how much liquor does a body have to take to remain in this here church?" *(The chamber reacts with laughter.)* To answer the gentleman of the First Circuit directly, I neither wish to prohibit the right of amendment nor see its unlimited use become the agent of our inability to enact needed legislation. I propose a compromise, namely that we limit the number of amendments to three per bill, and I move adoption at this time. *(The chamber reacts with whispered consultations.)*

SPEAKER: Is there a second?

VOICE: I second.

SPEAKER: In favor?

MAJORITY: Aye.

SPEAKER: Opposed?

ONE or TWO: No.

SPEAKER: It appears the motion is carried.

(The lights fade on the chamber and come up on SPEED off to one side.)

SPEED: Abe and Douglas become the cat and mouse of the entire session. Seems as soon as one got started on a thing, the other just naturally jumped up to oppose it. Take the debate over the Illinois canal. What with the riverboat traffic comin' up in such numbers from Missouri—a position I have always advocated—it just seemed natural to dig a canal connectin' the Illinois River with Lake Michigan at Chicago. That way, goods could go up the Hudson River from New York, across the Mohawk into Lake Erie and on to the Mississippi without never touchin' ocean water—or bein' hog-tied by an enemy blockade such as England had done in the eighteen twelve war. Wasn't nobody against the canal. The debate come over how Illinois was to pay for it.

(The lights fade on SPEED and come up on the legislature once again.)

SPEAKER: Recognize Mr. Douglas for the purpose of speaking to the issue of payment.

DOUGLAS: *(taking the podium)* Gentlemen of the Legislature, it is the result of my investigation into the matter before us that we do, indeed, have the legal right to withhold payment on the canal until such time as the tolls charged for its usage accrue to the total due. *(LINCOLN rises.)*

SPEAKER: For what purpose does the gentleman from New Salem rise?

LINCOLN: I'd like to ask a question, Mr. Speaker.

SPEAKER: Proceed, sir.

LINCOLN: Does the gentleman from the First Circuit plan to tell us from whom he would withhold this payment?

DOUGLAS: The agencies responsible for the construction of the canal.

LINCOLN: May I continue, Mr. Speaker?

SPEAKER: Is there objection? *(There is none.)* Proceed.

LINCOLN: I'd like to remind the gentleman that the "agencies" of which he speaks are in large measure ordinary hard-working men, many of whom have family obligations that can't wait until a toll quota is made.

DOUGLAS: My job, sir, was to ascertain the propriety of delayed payment, and that is what I have done. Such payment is entirely legal.

LINCOLN: Question is, Mr. Speaker, is it entirely moral? Thinkin' about Mr. Douglas's method of payment, I am reminded of my friend, John Armstrong, who saved all year for new boots only to have them made so small he couldn't get his feet into them. "Never mind," says he. "I'll get 'em on right enough after I wear 'em a day or two and stretch 'em out a little." *(The chamber laughs.)* Thing is, just how much stretchin' can we ask of an Illinois family? I reckon it'd be pretty hard for a man and wife and young'ns to stretch a hunger four, five, maybe six months while the flatboats do their business on the canal and we debate payment in Vandalia.

DOUGLAS: A brief question, Mr. Speaker.

SPEAKER: Proceed.

DOUGLAS: If the gentleman from New Salem does not wish to use the method of delayed payment, how does he then propose we construct this canal? Or does he wish the project abandoned and fail to recognize that in the pursuit of worthy endeavors, it sometimes happens that inconveniences are tolerated as they were tolerated by those brave men at Saratoga and Valley Forge and New Orleans who fought for a better life and gave us the great nation we enjoy today.

Earliest known photo of Lincoln: from a daguerreotype dated c. 1848.
LC-USZ62-4377

Photo of Act I, scene 9 from the original production of *The Prairie Man*. Lincoln is kneeling by the knoll where he and Ann had courted. "I'm sorry not to put these by your grave, Ann," he says, "but I feel this place is more proper." And Ann answers, "It isn't the years...it's what we do with them. I always felt you'd do so much with yours."

Charcoal sketch by Anthony Brunelli of the Rutledge Tavern in New Salem where Ann and Abe first met.

Photo of the original cast of *The Prairie Man* taken in August of 1990. From left to right: Steven Westlake as Joshua Speed, Elaine Kuracina Brehm as Mary Todd, Jim Hull as Abraham Lincoln, Kristin Gartner Hull as Ann Rutledge, and Dale Robinson as Stephen Douglas.

Photo of the set of Act II, scene 4 from the original production of *The Prairie Man*. The year is 1847. Lincoln has just been elected to the House of Representatives. Douglas is a member of the U.S. Senate. They are about to debate the issue of President Polk's involvement in the Mexican War. The rear-screen projection stage center is an actual sketch of the Capitol building made while its dome was still under construction.

Charcoal portrait of
Stephen Douglas
by Anthony Brunelli.

Charcoal portrait of
Joshua Speed
by Anthony Brunelli.

Lincoln's home in Springfield during the 1858 Senatorial campaign. Lincoln is the tall figure in white at the right of the front doorway. LC-USZ62-13682.

Photograph of the Springfield, Illinois street on which Lincoln had his law offices. LC-USZ62-13682.

Sketch of the Lincoln-Douglas debates dated 1858.
LC-USZ62-29291.

Photo of Act II, scene 6 of the original production of *The Prairie Man*.
There were, in actuality, seven debates between Lincoln and Douglas
beginning in Ottawa, Illinois and ending in Alton. People turned out by the
thousands to hear both men. In the play, all seven encounters are condensed
into one scene. The rear-screen projection stage center is an 1858 sketch of
the actual debate showing Lincoln speaking as Douglas listens.

Charcoal portrait of Mary Todd Lincoln by Anthony Brunelli. Mrs. Lincoln appears in her 1861 inaugural ball gown.

Lincoln with abolitionist preacher Isabella Baumfree (a.k.a. Sojourner Truth) displaying the bible given to him by the Negro population of Baltimore. Dated 1864.
LC-USZ62-16225.

Lincoln pictured with his cabinet at the first reading of the Emancipation Proclamation, July of 1862. Left to right: Secretary of War Stanton, Secretary of the Treasury Chase, Lincoln, Secretary of the Navy Wells, Secretary of the Interior Smith, Secretary of State Seward (seated), Postmaster General Blair, and Attorney General Bates.
LC-USZ62-2070.

LINCOLN: I appreciate the brevity. And the answer is, if inconvenience be the inescapable companion of progress, then let it be borne by those most able to bear it. I propose the shipping and mercantile companies who stand to profit from the canal advance the money to construct it, kind of an application fee. In exchange we might suspend their tolls for a year, and provide unlimited access. That way, Mr. Speaker, we build our canal, promote our commerce, but we also pay our people for an honest day's work.

SPEAKER: Do I hear a second?

VOICE: I second.

SPEAKER: In favor?

LEGISLATURE: Aye.

SPEAKER: Opposed? *(No one is opposed.)* Unanimously carried.

(He bangs his gavel as the men freeze and the lights fade on the chamber. SPEED appears alone in a spot.)

SPEED: Nothin' fired up the State Legislature that year more'n the issue of the National Bank, and it broke right straight down party lines, the Jackson Democrats bein' opposed and the Whigs bein' in favor. It was big doin's not only for Illinois, but the whole country, so when Abe and Douglas went at it, they was speakin' the minds of many folk far from the borders of Vandalia.

(The spot fades on SPEED as the Assembly chamber returns to view. DOUGLAS stands at the front of one bleacher section, LINCOLN in front of the other; between them the SPEAKER.)

DOUGLAS: I tell you, gentlemen, President Jackson is not an injudicious man. His opposition to the policies of the National Bank will result in the lowering of interest rates and the stability of the economy.

LINCOLN: If he persists, sir, in removin' all Federal revenue from the Bank, he surely will lower the interest. He'll also kill the Bank and create a panic among our foreign and domestic creditors the likes of which will drive us to ruin.

DOUGLAS: The Bank is a monopoly, sir, and must be discharged as such. It is an institution run by the privileged for the privileged. Its rates are approaching near usury and no Democrat is going to stand by and see that happen.

LINCOLN: I suspect if a few more Democrats stood on the Bank's Board of Directors, Mr. Jackson's opposition would lessen considerably.

DOUGLAS: Are you ascribing political motives to the President, sir?

LINCOLN: Why, Mr. Douglas. How could any thinkin' man accuse the President of political favoritism? When he fired all the Whigs and replaced them with good Democratic workers, we all knew it was purely for the good of the country. And now that he wants to take our money out of the National Bank and put it in the hands of more favored institutions, shall we say, no honorable man would question his motives.

DOUGLAS: If President Jackson is engaged in any impropriety, the law stands ever-ready to prosecute him.

LINCOLN: The law moves a tad slower, sir, than most people's lives. Like the boy caught stealin' from the church collection. "Better lay down that money, son, lest ye pay for it on the Day of Judgment." "By my faith, Parson, if the good Lord is goin' to credit me so long, I'll just take another handful." *(The chamber laughs.)*

DOUGLAS: Does the gentleman accuse President Jackson of theft? *(The chamber reacts by quieting to absolute silence.)*

SPEAKER: *(after an uneasy moment)* Mr. Douglas, do you wish to rephrase your remark?

DOUGLAS: No, sir, I do not! *(The chamber reacts.)*

SPEAKER: *(wrapping his gavel)* Gentlemen, please...Mr. Lincoln, you have the right to respond.

LINCOLN: Thank you, Mr. Speaker. I don't accuse anyone of anything, except maybe poor judgment. If the interest rates are too high, the way to deal with that is pass a law to lower them. Meanwhile we've got to protect the National Bank from any loss of revenue. This is simply not the time to fandango around with the nation's money. We got railroads bein' built and canals and people settlin' more and more land. Go and take away their hope of investment, you're goin' to kill off an opportunity comes only once to a nation's history. Mr. Speaker, I move that we show our support for the National Bank by establishing a State branch here in Illinois. And if Vandalia is too politically inconvenient, I suggest Springfield. *(The chamber murmurs.)*

DOUGLAS: I will oppose such a bank, Mr. Speaker! I will oppose it in the name of loyalty to our President, and I shall bend every effort to see that it is never incorporated!

SPEAKER: Mr. Douglas, we have a motion on the floor. Do I have a second?

VOICE: Second the motion.

SPEAKER: In favor.

DOUGLAS: Call for an individual vote, Mr. Speaker.

SPEAKER: So ordered. Alphabetically, then. Mr. Ames...

DOUGLAS: Closed ballot, Mr. Speaker.

SPEAKER: Is there objection? *(There is none.)* So ordered. This chamber stands adjourned for the purpose of casting written ballots on Mr. Lincoln's motion.

(The lights fade on center stage and pick up SPEED off to one side.)

SPEED: The legislature recessed February of thirty-five, and as Abe
passed through Springfield on the way home they was already layin'
the foundation of the bank he had fought to establish. All in all, it was
a good session for him, but he was anxious to return to the things he'd
left in New Salem...the things and the people.

*(SPEED exits.   The lights rise slowly on the wooded knoll. We are in
Scene 7.)*

SCENE 7

*(The oak bough tells us that it is now the Spring of 1835. ANN and
LINCOLN are seated against the tree. ANN is dressed warmly for Spring
and carries a handkerchief. As the lights come up, LINCOLN rises and
walks a few steps away.)*

LINCOLN: State of Illinois's givin' the Bar exam this summer and next.

ANN: Which do you think you'll take, Abe?

LINCOLN: I haven't thought much on it...*(He pauses and walks a few
steps more.)* John Stuart's got an openin' for a lawyer in his
Springfield office.

ANN: Has he said anything to you about it?

LINCOLN: We talked some in Vandalia...*(Again he pauses and takes
a few more steps.)* The store's doin' right well. Speed is a good
worker.

ANN: *(coughing)*...I know...I saw him at it this winter.

LINCOLN: You still got that. *(He points to his chest.)*

ANN: Most half the town's carryin' somethin'.

LINCOLN: You see Doctor Allen?

ANN: Twice, Abe. I'm fine.

LINCOLN: *(walking another few steps)* Chicago rail line's comin' south.

ANN: Is that the truth?

LINCOLN: *(turning to her)* Did you know that five years ago there was only thirty-two miles of rail in the entire country, and now there's nearly two thousand?

ANN: I guess that means a lot of opportunities for Illinois folk.

LINCOLN: *(taking another few steps as ANN coughs again)* The Springfield Bank is almost finished. They say it's only a matter of a couple weeks.

ANN: You did a real good job in Vandalia, Abe.

LINCOLN: *(turning to her)* Ann, I know I'm not a lawyer yet...

ANN: *(rising to him)* Mr. Lincoln, I'm not hurryin' off anywhere.

LINCOLN: Suppose I don't take the Bar exam until next August?

ANN: Suppose you don't?

LINCOLN: Or if Stuart hires someone else.

ANN: He won't.

LINCOLN: *(after a pause)* There isn't...

ANN: There's no one, Abe.

(They embrace as the lights fade on the knoll and pick up SPEED.)

SPEED: Coleman Smoot recovered from his fever, but many others in New Salem were not as strong. Wasn't until summer John Allen realized he had a full-blown crop of malaria on his hands. Abe got it, too, but rallied with doses of boneset tea and jalap. By July, the town had lost over a dozen. Then August come, and Ann turned for the worse. They brought in her cousin, McGrady, as nurse but there wasn't much McGrady could do. On August twenty-first, they rode into town to fetch Abe. It was dark by the time he got back to the Rutledge farm.

(The lights fade on SPEED and rise on the Rutledge parlour where ANN, covered with blankets, lies on a sofa. There are signs of illness—a basin, a cloth, etc.—about the bed.)

SCENE 8

(As the lights rise, LINCOLN is sitting in a chair by ANN'S side. They are both asleep.)

ANN: *(waking to see him)* Abe...*(He doesn't respond. She turns and reaches out for his hand.)* Abe...*(He stirs and takes her hand in his.)*

LINCOLN: I'm sorry, Ann. I must have drifted off...

ANN: You're so tired...

LINCOLN: I'm fine...How do you feel?

ANN: I think the fever's breaking.

LINCOLN: *(touching her head)* Why don't you try to get some more sleep?

ANN: I'd rather talk to you...*(after a pause)* You're not neglecting your law books?

LINCOLN: No, ma'am.

ANN: I haven't been able to help you study.

LINCOLN: There's plenty of time for that. I've decided to wait until next summer for the exam. We've got a whole year to study.

ANN: I think we've worn away most of the grass by our tree.

LINCOLN: We'll find another tree.

ANN: No. I don't want another. I want it to be our tree...always.

LINCOLN: I love you, Miss Rutledge.

ANN: I love you, Mr. Lincoln.

(The lights fade on the parlour and reappear on SPEED.)

SPEED: Ann died on the twenty-fifth of August, eighteen thirty-five and was buried not far from the edge of town. As for Abe, no one seen him after the funeral. He took a job surveyin' deep in the woods, leavin' me to tend the store. And he didn't bring nothin' with him 'cept his tools. Not even the law books. September and October come and went, and still there was no sign of him.

(The lights fade on SPEED and rise on the knoll. It is November, 1835.)

SCENE 9

(LINCOLN enters carrying his surveying tools in one hand. In the other he holds a bouquet of prairie flowers. He puts the tools down by the edge of the knoll and walks slowly to the base of the tree, kneels, places the flowers down gently, and rises with his head still bowed.)

LINCOLN: I'm sorry not to put these by your grave, Ann, but I just feel this place is more proper. It's prairie heather and some laurel I picked down by where they're bringin' in the new rail spur...Joshua'll be mighty pleased. He's finally gettin' his train to Chicago. I suppose I'll never hear the end of it now. He'll want me to go to Vandalia and talk up a storm second term for a connection to Springfield. *(He walks away from the tree a few paces.)* Ann, I don't want to go back to Vandalia. I don't want to read any law books or take any exams next summer. Who needs it anyway? Fella can drive himself crazy with ambition. Study this! Study that! What for? I know plenty of folks put in a crop or two, raise their children, and just grow old together. They're happy, Ann. Just growin' old and havin' each other...

(When he finishes, he kneels by the flowers and with great care begins to plant them at the base of the tree. As he does so, ANN appears near him but behind his line of sight. She is in a Sunday dress and bathed in a white spot. LINCOLN freezes as the lights dim on him. It is clear that he is unable to see or hear her.)

ANN: Everyone grows old, Abe. There's nothing special in just growin' old. It isn't the years...it's what we do with them. I always felt you'd do so much with yours.

(The lights dim on her and come up on LINCOLN who rises with his tools and exits in the opposite direction as the set fades to black. Act I is over.)

ACT II

SCENE 1

(SPEED, bedecked in a formal suit, enters from one side. He is clearly uncomfortable, tugging at a collar and tie which are apparently too small for him.)

SPEED: I hate these things! Can't see why people's got to put 'emselves in a straightjacket just to visit the same folks they see every day. *(He finally undoes the tie and opens the collar.)* There! Now maybe I can talk to you in peace. It's eighteen hundred and forty. Ann's been five years gone, and Abe...he moved into Springfield. Passed them law exams of his and got himself a partner down by the Court House. Still heavy into politics, but he don't travel to Vandalia anymore. Remember that Springfield bank he helped start? Well, the damn thing made so much money they moved the State Capitol next door to it. Our President's Mr. William Henry Harrison, and Steve

Douglas is a judge on the Illinois Supreme Court. Oh yes, *(he begins to walk to stage center)* and we're on our way to the annual shindig of the Illinois State Legislature. Don't mind the damn thing. I just wish they'd let a fella dress a little more natural.

(He enters the Court House—which comes into view dotted with couples dancing in formal attire—and greets LINCOLN who walks alone downstage. DOUGLAS approaches with a woman on his arm. She is not at all like Ann—ample where Ann was delicate, dark where Ann was fair— but she is feminine and attractive. DOUGLAS acknowledges SPEED who passes upstage and blends into the crowd.)

DOUGLAS: Abe...oh Abe...

LINCOLN: *(turning to them)* Good evening, Steve.

DOUGLAS: Abe, I'd like you to meet someone.

LINCOLN: Whig or Democrat?

MARY: I don't believe I've made up my mind yet, Mr. Lincoln.

DOUGLAS: Abe, this is Miss Mary Todd...from Kentucky.

LINCOLN: Pleased to meet you, ma'am. *(He nods politely.)*

DOUGLAS: Her father is Robert Todd.

LINCOLN: The banker...

MARY: Father is many things, Mr. Lincoln. A man of many ambitions.

LINCOLN: I apologize, Miss Todd. I know him only as a financier.

MARY: No offense taken, sir. *(She curtsies.)*

DOUGLAS: Abe here would give you to think he doesn't hold much with ambition.

MARY: Is that so, Mr. Lincoln?

DOUGLAS: But don't let the backwoods charm fool you, Mary. Before he's done, he'll outrank us all.

LINCOLN: Not true, ma'am. I expect it's Steve's goin' to set us the pace.

DOUGLAS: He's only covering his tracks. Remember, I told you he comes from the prairie.

MARY: Do you gentlemen always go on like this?

LINCOLN: Always.

DOUGLAS: It's the only way he has of showing he likes me.

MARY: I see.

DOUGLAS: Abe, I've got some business with Mr. Fell. Would you look after Miss Todd for a bit? Mary, I hope you'll forgive me.

MARY: Not at all, Mr. Douglas. *(DOUGLAS exits. MARY takes LINCOLN'S arm.)* I expect it'd be cooler by the river. If you'll escort me, I promise not to be too much of a burden.

LINCOLN: Whatever you'd like, Miss Todd.

(They walk to the dock as the courthouse fades to black. The moonlight reflects off the Sangamon as it did once before.)

MARY: Is it really true you and Stephen...Mr. Douglas...always carry on?

LINCOLN: I'm afraid so. And most of it on the floor of the Legislature. We've been goin' at it near six years now.

MARY: But off the floor you're friends.

LINCOLN: Let's say we have a tolerable respect for each other.

MARY: Well, I hope you're friends...because I think Mr. Douglas is destined for important things.

LINCOLN: I trust there's more to friendship than measurin' a man's destiny.

MARY: Why certainly. I didn't mean to imply anything to the contrary...only...

LINCOLN: Only what, Miss Todd?

MARY: Only destiny makes it a bit more compelling. Don't you agree?

LINCOLN: I never really gave it much thought.

MARY: A man of your ambitions?

LINCOLN: My ambitions? *(He laughs.)* Sometimes I think the extent of my ambition is just to get out of bed without bumpin' myself on the ceilin'.

MARY: Rather modest for a highly respected Assemblyman.

LINCOLN: I'm afraid that's all a lot of political folderol.

MARY: I don't think so, Mr. Lincoln.

LINCOLN: Why of course it is.

MARY: I believe there's a look about men of destiny. I think it attracts people of its own accord...sometimes even without the knowledge of the men themselves.

LINCOLN: Where ever did you learn that, Miss Todd?

MARY: My father, Mr. Lincoln. He rose up a long way from the time our ancestors first came here...from humble schooling to an Army Captain and State Senator and finally President of the Bank of Kentucky. He's a man of destiny, and he taught me to see it in others.

LINCOLN: *(after a pause)* I wonder what advice he'd have for Mr. Douglas.

MARY: I believe he'd encourage his ambition and discourage his propensity for argument.

LINCOLN: *(laughing)* Wait until Stephen hears that!

MARY: Oh, I already mentioned it to him.

LINCOLN: *(still laughing)* You did!

MARY: And he thought it would suit you even better.

LINCOLN: *(laughing)* Me! Why me?

MARY: I expect he considers you a man of destiny, too, Mr. Lincoln.

LINCOLN: He considers everyone he argues with a man of destiny.

MARY: No, I believe he's quite correct, Mr. Lincoln. I believe you'll do just about anything you want in this life.

LINCOLN: I don't even know how many years this life holds, Miss Todd. *(He walks away.)*

MARY: It's not the years, Mr. Lincoln. It's what you decide to make of them. *(LINCOLN turns abruptly.)* Why...I believe I've said something to offend you.

LINCOLN: *(recovering)* No...no, not at all.

MARY: You look like you've just seen a ghost.

LINCOLN: Perhaps I have, Miss Todd...

MARY: *(taking his arm)* Shall we go back in, Mr. Lincoln?

(They walk toward center stage as the lights fade to black.)

(SPEED appears in a spot to the side of the stage.)

SPEED: Mary didn't return to Kentucky that summer. Instead she took lodgin' at the big Edwards' house right there in Springfield and become a regular part of the town. Mr. Edwards, bein' a member of the Illinois Legislature, there was a fair stream of politicians in and out of the place, and him bein' a Whig, there was many an excuse for Mary and Abe to meet. Didn't seem like the two of 'em minded much, either.

(The spot dims as SPEED exits. Once more the old oak becomes visible. We are at the wooded knoll. Several months have passed. It is August of 1840. A bank of flowers gilds the tree telling us that LINCOLN has been there from time to time. He enters to place yet another garland on the spot. We are in Scene 2.)

SCENE 2

(LINCOLN kneels at the tree, gently puts his flowers among the others, and rises.)

LINCOLN: It's five years today, Ann, since you left us, and I don't feel any further from you than when you were here. Closer, maybe...Joshua says there's some folks united more by separation than marriage. I guess that's us. But Ann, I've met this woman. *(He makes his way down the knoll as ANN appears from behind the tree dressed as she was before. During the following they do not look at each other or react to each other's presence.)* She's from Kentucky. Lexington. Very well off. Her Daddy's a big bank President...

ANN: Don't be afraid, Abe. Don't be ashamed of it.

LINCOLN: And she thinks I could run for Congress, Ann.

ANN: Tell me what she's like, Abe. Is she pretty?

LINCOLN: She's got all sorts of ambitions. Sometimes she thinks so fast, I can't keep up with her. She knows so many people. And not just in Illinois or Kentucky, but Washington and New York and Philadelphia. Important people. People of influence...I...

ANN: She sounds just fine, Abe. She sounds wonderfully good for you.

LINCOLN: ...I'm pledged to marry her, Ann. I'm pledged to her and I don't know if I love her. Sometimes she can be so damned stubborn. Righteous and haughty. You know what Joshua says about her? He says it was presumptuous of her to spell her name with two D's when one was good enough for God. And damn it—he's right. She's got that way with her...I don't feel for her like I did with us...but she has a sense of purpose kindles something in me, Ann, and I can't stay away from it...I don't know...I come here and talk to you like I expect you to walk out from behind that tree over there and tell me what to do. *(He laughs gently.)* You were the only person ever did that and made me feel good, Miss Rutledge...well...somewhere I guess you're listening...

(He looks about a last time and exits. ANN walks to where he has placed the flowers and picks them up.)

ANN: You always bring such pretty flowers, Mr. Lincoln. It's important to have someone to bring flowers to. I hope you bring them to your new lady.

(When she is done, the lights dim to black.)

SCENE 3

(It is early May of 1846. The lights rise on the Illinois State Whig Convention where nominations for Congress are being conducted. The bleachers are filled with men and women of the party. In the front row to one side sit LINCOLN and MARY. In her arms MARY holds a son, barely a few months old. At stage center the Whig SPEAKER presides at his podium.)

SPEAKER: The chair will entertain questions from the Convention floor regarding the nomination of Mr. Abraham Lincoln for the office of Congressman from the Springfield district. *(The crowd applauds.)* Mr. Lincoln, would you mind joinin' me on the podium? *(LINCOLN moves to center stage amid cheers of encouragement. The SPEAKER wraps his gavel calling the hall to order.)* From Mr. Giles of Petersburg.

GILES: *(rising from the bleachers)* I don't suppose there's none of us here ain't seen your charmin' wife and baby sittin' with you, Mr. Lincoln...

LINCOLN: Thank you for the observation, Mr. Giles.

GILES: My question is, with the young'ns and Washington a long way's off, don't you think the job'd be a might hard on your family?

LINCOLN: I'd planned to take them with me, but maybe Mary could tell you better...

(MARY rises, still holding the baby.)

MARY: Good evening, Mr. Giles.

GILES: Good evening, ma'am. I don't mean no disrespects...

MARY: And none taken, sir. None taken, I assure you. You have a perfect right to know how I and my family might affect my husband's representation of you.

GILES: Thank you, ma'am.

MARY: The truth is, as my husband has said, we plan to travel with him, and when Washington—if Washington—wears a bit thin, I plan to stay with my family in Kentucky. They are quite well able to care for me and the children until my husband's business is done. I hope that answers your questions.

GILES: Right well, Mrs. Lincoln. Thank you very much.

(MARY and GILES sit amid polite applause.)

SPEAKER: Mr. Robert Thomas of Galesburg.

THOMAS: *(rising)* Mr. Lincoln, as you know, the Democrats have nominated the Reverend Peter Cartwright to run against you.

LINCOLN: I know him well.

THOMAS: Then you must also know that he has attacked you as a man not given to God or the Church. A man who holds drunkards as good as Christians...

LINCOLN: Yes, I've heard, Mr. Thomas.

THOMAS: And that you refuse to honor the doctrine of the Church that a soul may go to heaven on the Day of Judgment! *(There is an awkward silence.)* How do you respond to the Reverend Cartwright, Mr. Lincoln?

LINCOLN: That I am not a member of any Christian Church is true. But I have never denied the truth of the Scriptures nor the power of the God who made and preserves us all. I suppose the greatest difference between me and the Reverend Cartwright is that I do not compel others—as he does—to see religion in my own personal way. I do not think any of us has the right to insult the feelings or injure the morals of his brothers. Those are subjects left between each man and his Maker—or what did our fathers and grandfathers come here for?...Now as for where I am going on the day of my judgment, you be kind enough to tell Reverend Cartwright that I'm going to Congress! Lord willing!

(There is applause and laughter as THOMAS sits.)

SPEAKER: I believe I see James Shields with a question. Mr. Shields?

SHIELDS: *(rising)* Mr. Lincoln, these are perilous times. We got a Democrat in the White House seems intent on annexing every territory west of the Mississippi and south of the Rio Grande.

LINCOLN: Doesn't sound like he's much of a friend of yours, Mr. Shields. *(mild laughter)*

SHIELDS: Well he sure as hell ain't a Whig, Mr. Lincoln. *(laughter)* What I want to know is, how do you stand on his notion to take Mexico and them other territories by force?

LINCOLN: Mexico and "them other territories" don't belong to us. I learned right well enough when I was young not to dip my hand into a bear's winter larder—unless I didn't especially mind losing my hand. Protecting our settlers in the Texas territory is one thing. Buying up new lands so we stretch to the Pacific? Well, okay, if that's our destiny. We'll pay good money for 'em. But Mexico isn't ours to buy or take. I do not stand with President Polk on that issue.

DELEGATE 1: *(rising, unrecognized, in a military uniform)* What'll you do if the President sends General Taylor across the Rio Grande?

LINCOLN: If he does that, they'll be war.

DELEGATE 1: You didn't answer the question, sir.

LINCOLN: There are no simple answers to the question of war.

DELEGATE 2: *(also unrecognized)* Will you or will you not support President Polk?

LINCOLN: No. I will not. But...

DELEGATE 3: *(amid some commotion now)* That's practically a statement of treason...

(The delegates begin to react aloud with comments of disapproval. The SPEAKER wraps his gavel calling them to order.)

SPEAKER: Gentlemen...gentlemen...(The hall quiets down.) Gentlemen, I believe we owe Mr. Lincoln the opportunity to answer us. Why don't you all just calm down and be seated. *(The delegates sit.)* Mr. Lincoln, the floor is yours, I believe.

LINCOLN: You ask me would I support President Polk if he were to provoke a war with Mexico. And I tell you that any unprovoked war is wrong. I served in a war, did I not, Captain Shields?

SHIELDS: *(rising)* You did, Mr. Lincoln. In my own command at the Black Hawk War.

LINCOLN: And though it was no great conflict, neither was it the pleasantry of a gentleman's afternoon, was it, Captain?

SHIELDS: War's war, Mr. Lincoln. A fact I fear some of these men don't know. *(He sits.)*

LINCOLN: And the Mexican people are not an isolated Indian tribe fighting for a few acres of hunting land.

DELEGATE 1: *(rising uncontrollably)* You still got no right to turn your back on American soldiers in the field.

LINCOLN: I don't know you, son. What's your name?

DELEGATE 1: Jed Rutledge, if it makes any difference.

LINCOLN: *(There is a noticeable silence.)* From New Salem?

RUTLEDGE: No, Freeport. But I got kin used to live in New Salem.

LINCOLN: *(tenderly)* No right-thinking man in the Congress of the United States, Jed, would turn his back on our boys in the field, and if God gives us to war with Mexico and I have to vote for the bullets to do it, I will. *(Rutledge sits.)* But that's not what you asked me, son. You asked me if I wanted to support a war south of the Rio Grande, and I tell you such a war would be wrong. Abjectly wrong. Politically, socially, militarily wrong. What would be its purpose? We can barely settle the lands we've got now. The Northwest Louisiana Territory...the new Oregon Territory...we've hardly enough people to cut the timber there...build the homes and farm the crops. No sir, Jed. Don't ask me to send you off to die at the point of a Spanish bayonet with my hat held high a-wavin' in the May sun. But if you go, boy, I'll not turn my back on you. You'll have my vote...and you'll have my prayers.

(There is a long silence before SHIELDS rises again.)

SHIELDS: What'll happen if there is a war with Mexico, Mr. Lincoln?

LINCOLN: I don't rightly know, Jim. I expect a lot of our men will be killed...and a lot more Mexicans will be killed. I think it unlikely that we would lose such a war. We'll probably win some sort of settlement and fix the Texas border at the Rio Grande...but that's not what worries me. It's what will happen to the Texas Territory once the war is over. This Manifest Destiny of ours is just the surface of what we've got to face in the years ahead. The real issue, my friend, is slavery. For once we acquire and settle new land—whether it be in Kansas, Nebraska, Oregon, or Texas—we've got to decide if it's going to be slave land or free land...and that might...in the long run...mean a lot more blood than what could be shed in Mexico. No matter who goes to Congress in the fall, this nation is headed for trying times and it occurs to me as I speak here that the burdens of the office may be more than any one man would wish to bear...

(The lights fade slowly on a silent hall. SPEED appears in a spot off to one side.)

SPEED: Eleven days after Abe received the nomination for Congress, President Polk declared war on Mexico. Illinois sent eight thousand men to fight, of whom three thousand seven hundred 'n twenty crossed the Texas Gulf and landed on the shores of the Rio Grande. Jim Shields was appointed brigadier general of the Illinois regiment. He was to die a soldier of valor, taking a bullet in the lungs at the battle of Cerro Gordo. They shipped his body home along with the remains of Jed Rutledge just about election time.

(The lights fade to black.)

SCENE 4

(It is early Winter 1847. As the lights come up we see a corridor of the Capitol Building in Washington, D.C. To one side is the House chamber; to the other, the Senate. Legislators and aides make their way out of each, collect into groups and exit amid the clatter of political talk. As the corridor clears, LINCOLN emerges from the House chamber, DOUGLAS from the Senate. Both are reading intently. They graze shoulders as they pass.)

DOUGLAS: *(looking up)* Beg your pardon...Congressman.

LINCOLN: Good morning, Stephen.

DOUGLAS: They got you studying pretty hard, Abe?

LINCOLN: No more'n necessary.

DOUGLAS: I got war figures here. What about you?

LINCOLN: Same.

DOUGLAS: Senate's asking for thirty-five million.

LINCOLN: You won't get it. The Democrats may have the Senate, but you'll fall short in the House.

DOUGLAS: Not if we get some help from the other side of the aisle.

LINCOLN: That sounds mighty like a job offer, Mr. Douglas.

DOUGLAS: Consider it from whence it comes, sir.

LINCOLN: Is the President so desperate for new land he'd send you to fetch the help of a Freshman Whig?

DOUGLAS: Don't be unfair to the man, Abe. Mr. Polk is also concerned with our boys down there.

LINCOLN: That's right decent of him, Steve. Considering we've already taken more than ten thousand dead.

DOUGLAS: We've also taken possession of a good deal of new territory.

LINCOLN: Now who was it said that? Frederick the Great? "Take possession now and negotiate afterwards?"

DOUGLAS: I said it. Yesterday. In the Senate.

LINCOLN: Oh.

DOUGLAS: And what's wrong with a little Manifest Destiny?

LINCOLN: The cost is too high, Steve. I more than suspect the President is deeply conscious of being in the wrong...

DOUGLAS: I don't think so...

LINCOLN: No. He feels the blood of this war. He has to, and he longs to be at peace.

DOUGLAS: Peace'll be all the faster, Abe, if we get the support we need. Will you help us?

LINCOLN: In exchange for what?

DOUGLAS: The President's word that no Mexican territory will enter the Union as slave land?

LINCOLN: I'll shuck your corn, you shuck mine.

DOUGLAS: Put it any way you like.

LINCOLN: I'd like to sleep on it.

DOUGLAS: Take all the time you need. Goodnight, Mr. Congressman.

(DOUGLAS exits. LINCOLN stares, melancholy, at his papers and walks slowly back into the House Chamber.)

LINCOLN: Good night, Stephen.

(The lights dim and come up again showing a passage of time. In the corridor, groups of legislators appear arguing over the current business. They ad lib their concerns with lines like "We won't vote for that;" "It's not an acceptable compromise;" "The House will never support you," etc. LINCOLN and DOUGLAS emerge from the groups. As the rest exit into the House and Senate chambers, the two men walk slowly toward each other.)

DOUGLAS: The President thanks you. Twenty-seven million was more than he expected from the Whigs.

LINCOLN: I didn't do it for him.

DOUGLAS: No? Then for whom?

LINCOLN: Say it was for Jim Shields' widow.

DOUGLAS: Well, he thanks you just the same.

LINCOLN: Alright then. It's time for your bushel of corn.

(LINCOLN takes a paper from his coat pocket.)

DOUGLAS: What's this?

LINCOLN: You know Dave Wilmot?

DOUGLAS: Congressman from Pennsylvania.

LINCOLN: Dave'll pass this in the House...*(He hands it to DOUGLAS who reads it intently.)*...but we'll need your help to get it through the Senate.

DOUGLAS: *(reading)* But this says any territory taken or purchased from Mexico to be free of slavery.

LINCOLN: That's what it says.

DOUGLAS: Taken maybe. But purchased? I don't know, Abe. That's not what I promised. Suppose fifty years from now we want to build a rail line to Southern California?

LINCOLN: Suppose we do?

DOUGLAS: We'd have to buy the Mexican land between West Texas and the Coast. *(He hands the paper back.)*

LINCOLN: Then we'll buy it.

DOUGLAS: And admit it to the Union as a free state?

LINCOLN: That's what we have in mind, Senator.

DOUGLAS: The South will never go for it.

LINCOLN: Why not? They've already changed the balance of power with this damned war. They'll have more representation than they know what to do with. Who cares if sometime in the future there's another free state?

DOUGLAS: You're not making my life any easier, Mr. Congressman.

LINCOLN: It was your idea, Stephen. The whole bargain was your idea. I was dead set against this war, but I voted for every single appropriations bill just to keep my word to you.

DOUGLAS: Don't get excited, Abe.

LINCOLN: You know it's not our fight down there. We got good boys North and South dyin' on land doesn't belong to us. It's the Mexicans defendin' their firesides and it surely pleasures me little to know I'm helping to pay for their killin'. The only reason I do it is because it pleasures me even less to see any blood spilled in the cause of slavery. You gave your word, Stephen. Now keep it.

DOUGLAS: *(exiting into the Senate chamber)* I'll do my best, Abe.

(LINCOLN stares after him, tucks the paper slowly into his coat, and exits into the House. As he does so, the lights dim. A spot comes up on SPEED.)

SPEED: Douglas's best was none too good. And there was some said he might've tried a little harder. The war ended and we fixed the Texas border at the Rio Grande, like Abe said we would, with most of the new territory eventually comin' in as slave land. It cost twenty-seven thousand American lives to do it—and God knows how many Mexicans. Back home, folks wasn't too happy with Abe. They saw his speakin' against the war as an insult to our boys in the field. When election time come round again, Abe decided not to run. Smart. He went back to the law and kept close to Springfield and his family. In eighteen fifty, Mary presented him with his third son, Billy, and three years later little Thomas Todd who he come to call Tad. *(The lights dim.)*

SCENE 5

(It is now 1856, August, the twenty-first anniversary of Ann's death. We are at the knoll. LINCOLN enters with flowers, kneels at the tree and prays. He has gotten older. His movements are slower; his voice more deliberate and melancholy.)

LINCOLN: *(rising)* I hardly know where to begin, Ann. It's been so long, I mean. Billy's near six now, and Tad...good Lord, he's clear up to my waist...Mary's fine...she made a good wife, Ann. She's a good mother to the boys...

(He pauses and walks away. ANN appears from behind the tree. She is unchanged. The passing years have taken their toll only on LINCOLN. She walks near to him.)

ANN: You look tired, Abe. And a little sad. Are things not going well?

LINCOLN: Joshua's married. Been a papa for a few years now. He found himself a girl in Kentucky. He's back there with a business...doin' real well.

ANN: It must be lonely for you in Springfield.

LINCOLN: Only thing is, I miss him...remember how the three of us used to sit around the stove at old man Offutt's?

ANN: What's on your mind, Abe?

LINCOLN: Lord, but those were happy days. I didn't know it near as much then as now, but...they were surely happy days.

(He walks away, lost for how to express himself.)

ANN: Tell me, Abe. Is it that the nation's doin' poorly? I can see those things where I am. I can see a lot.

(He turns and speaks suddenly as if a dam has broken.)

LINCOLN: I can't stay with them any longer, Ann. People I've known all my life...grew up with...planted fields with. I don't know what's come over them, but as soon as the talk gets to slavery, they become...I don't know...crazy folk. Their minds twistin', turnin' like someone's jabbin' at 'em with a hot blade...

ANN: It's a changing world, Abe...

LINCOLN: Men I politicked with twenty years in the Whig Party...stood shoulder to shoulder with in the Black Hawk War. I thought we were fightin' for the same things, Ann.

ANN: What do they want you to do, Abe?

LINCOLN: I can't conscience the extension of slavery, Ann. I just can't do it. It was all I had to support Zach Taylor after the Mexican War, and when he became President I wasn't a bit happy about it. Now Douglas is stirrin' up the people with this Kansas-Nebraska Act...

ANN: You knew that was bound to happen...

LINCOLN: I mean people's killin' each other out there in Kansas. There isn't a black man for a hundred miles and they're burnin' each other's farms and murderin' each other's wives. For what? So Steve Douglas can run for President? *(He turns and walks toward the tree, calmer now, and kneels once more beside the flowers.)* It's funny how these things never seem to need tendin'. I just stick 'em in the ground and years later they're here, strong as ever, pretty as ever. *(He pauses.)* They're forming a new party, Ann. Call themselves Republicans. They want me to run against Douglas for the Senate...against a lot of my old friends...

(He tucks a few flowers lovingly into the ground, rises slowly, and exits.)

ANN: The flowers are strong because you know how to plant them, Abe. You always knew how.

(When she is finished, the lights dim slowly to black.)

SCENE 6

(SPEED appears in a spot off to one side.)

SPEED: By 1858, Abe had joined the Republican Party and agreed to run against Douglas for the U.S. Senate. It was mighty big doin's for a prairie state like Illinois, let me tell you. Steve Douglas was a man of national standin', and the issue of slavery a matter of national importance. There was more than prairie eyes watchin'. It got so the two men decided to debate their differences in public—winner take all. Actually there was seven debates startin' in Ottawa, Illinois and endin' at Alton a few weeks before the election. People turned out by the wagonload to see the great contest. Fifteen thousand in Freeport, twelve thousand in Charleston, and there was twenty thousand stood in a cold October rain to hear them in Galesburg...The debates began near twenty-three years to the day that Ann died.

(He exits as the lights fade. In a single spot DOUGLAS becomes visible center stage.)

DOUGLAS: I'd like to start by saying that Mr. Lincoln is a very able and a very honest man. He is the strongest man of his party and the best stump speaker in the West. I shall have my hands full with him. Yessir! Of all the damned rascals about, Mr. Lincoln is surely the most able...But Mr. Lincoln boldly and clearly advocates a war of sections! A war of the North against the South! A war of free states against slave states! A war of extermination to be continued relentlessly until the one or the other shall be subdued and all the states shall either become slave or become free! *(He pauses.)* Now I want you good people to know that in any remarks I make on this platform, I mean nothing disrespectful to Mr. Lincoln. I have known him nearly twenty-five years, and there were many points of sympathy between us when we first got acquainted. We were both poor, both struggling uphill to make something better of ourselves. He had come to the Illinois Legislature from the humble life of a grocer and surveyor. I had come as a teacher and cabinet maker—specializing, as they said, in bureaus and secretaries. Yessir, we had much in common, and there was a sympathy between us. Yet I found him to be a man of public moods. He served with me in 1836 but then submerged and was lost sight of. In 1846 when Wilmot introduced his celebrated Proviso and a tornado of controversy swept over the country, Lincoln again turned up as a member of Congress from the Sangamon district. I was then in the Senate of the United States and glad to welcome my old friend and companion. But while he was there he took opposition to the Mexican War. Took the enemy's side against his own country! He oughtn't to have done that, for when he returned from Washington you good folks visited your indignation upon him and forced him to retire from public life—forgotten by his old friends. Now he sees the winds of controversy arising again, and he has decided to come up once more just in time to make something out of this Abolitionist fury. Well, if a man stands up and repeats and asserts and reasserts that two and two do not make four, I know nothing in the power of argument that can stop him. I can only commend him to look at the action of others. I say to Mr. Lincoln, the Supreme Court has already spoken on this issue! Mr. Justice Taney has called Dred Scott a slave and struck down the articles of the Missouri Compromise, and I say whoever resists the decision of the highest court in this land aims a deadly blow at our whole system of government! I thank God the time has not yet come when a handful of traitors in our camp can turn the great state of Illinois—with all her glorious history and traditions—into a negro-worshipping, negro-equality community! *(He walks a bit to let his words die away.)* For what do they wish this equality? So that a black man may earn what a white man earns? Or a black woman hold the charms of a white woman? It cannot be done. The blacks are simply not the equal of the whites. That has been clear from the beginning of this nation. The signers of the Declaration of Independence referred to the white race alone and not to the African when they declared that all men were created equal. Moreover, they were speaking of British subjects on this continent being equal to British subjects born and residing in Great Britain. *(He pauses again.)* But let us not have any misunderstanding here. Just because I do not consider the black man my equal, I do not advocate his mistreatment. Humanity requires and Christianity demands that we extend to every inferior being all the privileges, immunities, and advantages which can be granted to them—consistent with the security of society, that is. And I say this not only of the present society of America, but of her future as well—a future, my friends, destined to bring greatness. Why America swarms as does a hive of bees. In less than fifteen years, I predict every foot of vacant land between the Atlantic and Pacific oceans owned by the United States will be occupied! And just as fast as our interests and destiny require more land, I say I am for it! And when we acquire it, I say we leave the people on it free to decide as they wish about slavery and every other question. I say let every state mind its business and leave its neighbors alone! If we stand by that principle, then Mr. Lincoln will find that we can exist forever divided into free and slave states! Stand by that great principle and we can go on as we have done, increasing in wealth, in population, in power until we shall be the admiration and terror of the world! Until we make this continent one ocean-bound republic!

(The spot dims on DOUGLAS and comes up on LINCOLN who wears his top hat and carries an umbrella.)

LINCOLN: You know it rained in Galesburg, and they told us it was goin' to rain again today, so Mary allowed as how I'd have to wear my hat and bring my chute. *(He holds out his hand as if to feel for moisture.)* Not a drop. *(He removes his hat.)* Well, I reckon there's about as much to predicting the weather as there is to predicting politics. Now if you'll just let me set these down...*(He walks to one* *side and deposits his garb offstage. The spot follows him in all of this.)* Not that I'm ungrateful for the hat. Hats can hide a multitude of problems...*(He makes his way back to stage center, talking as he goes.)*...which in my case is right fortunate. For example, it has been noted that the size of my nose is such that it arrives in town fully one day before the rest of me. And that's hardly all. Once a woman said to me, "Good Lord but you're the ugliest man I ever saw!" "Yes, Madame," I replied, "but I can't help it." "No, I suppose not," she argued. "However, you might at least stay home!" Yessir. Looks can be mighty important to people. Did you know, for instance, that since 1854, a hog and a black man tend to look alike in the new Nebraska Territory? No, it's true. Just ask Judge Douglas. "Inasmuch as you do not object to my taking my hog to Nebraska," he has often said, "I must not object to your taking your slave." *(He pauses.)* I suppose that makes sense, assumin' no differences between hogs and slaves. But it's a right hard assumption when you're lookin' at the two of them. Don't see how a person could rightly make such an assumption. Which is why, good friends, I supported the Missouri Compromise and opposed the Judge's Kansas-Nebraska Act. According to the way I see it, there is more than passing difference between a hog and a black man. So while I would allow hogs to be treated like property above the Missouri line, I don't rightly hold the same for black folk. And for that matter, I don't believe Judge Douglas does either—really—because his law doesn't say that slavery is allowable in the new territories. Just that the new residents can vote to decide what they want. *(Again he pauses.)* And that brings up an inconsistency with Mr. Douglas I always wanted to ask him about. He says he supports the Supreme Court's decision in the Dred Scott case— that as a slave, Dred Scott is to be considered property anywhere he goes, south of Missouri or north of it. Well, fine. But now if Mr. Scott is a slave in the North, then how would it ever be possible for the settlers in the new northern territories to vote him a free man? Judge Douglas says the new territories should be able to decide such questions. Fine again. But how can they if the question has already been decided for them? Can't have it both ways. Can't say a man's a slave and a free man at one and the same time. Can't play with words like that. It's akin to the peddler so skilled at twistin' the meaning of things he could extract the price of a chestnut horse for the sale of a horse chestnut. I'm sorry, Stephen, but that's the truth of it. I don't believe you can say slavery is wrong here and right there. You can't say you'll allow it here and oppose it there. "I'm against slavery," the good Judge declares. But he won't oppose it in the free states because it's not there. And he won't oppose it in the slave states because it *is* there! He won't oppose it in politics because it'll make a fuss. He won't oppose it in the pulpit because it's not religion! Where then, Judge, would you have us oppose it? *(He pauses to think for a moment.)* Personally, I oppose it everywhere, for where there is slavery it has been first introduced without law. It is a monstrous injustice—inconsistent in every aspect with the intent of this democracy. We began by saying "all men are created equal." We now practically read it "all men are created equal except Negroes." Soon it shall read "all men are created equal except Negroes, foreigners and Catholics." When it comes to this, I should prefer emigrating to some country which makes no pretense of loving liberty. A country where despotism can be taken pure—without the base alloy of hypocrisy. Now I know you people. I was raised with you people. We built our homes together, plowed our fields together. You're good people. God-fearing people. You know what's right, and you know what's not. You know we pushed the Indians from their homes, and you surely know we have turned on others not fortunate enough to come over as early as we and our forefathers. And what does Judge Douglas say of this? Well, in effect, he scolds the black man, the Jew, the Irishman for not being born here. And what can they reply? *(with an Irish brogue)* "Faith, Mr. Senator, I wanted to be, but me mother wouldn't let me." No, I must say I'm against slavery. And when I say that—when they call me an abolitionist—I know the pain some slave owners must be feeling. When Southerners tell me they are no more responsible for slavery than I, I cannot take issue with them. When they say the practice exists and will be difficult to get rid of, I can understand and appreciate their concern. Theirs is a universal anxiety. It cannot be ignored. They in fact have the legal right to hold what they hold. I have never denied that. But it is all the more reason why I must oppose the extension of slavery into new lands, new territories, and free states. As an injustice, it cannot be allowed to spread. Judge Douglas says the Declaration of Independence referred only to white men of British descent. I reckon there might be a few of you out there with French or German blood could take issue with that. I reckon you'd be mighty against French slaves or German slaves. It's not the color of the slave at all, but the principle of slavery which is the injustice. The principle which says, "You work and you toil and earn bread, and I'll eat it." No matter in what shape it comes, whether from the mouth of a king or from one race of man as an apology for enslaving another, it is the same tyrannical principle. And don't you see that if it can be used to enslave a black man today, it can be used to enslave a white man tomorrow? Judge Douglas tells you I want to destroy the Union with this kind of talk, that I say what I'm a-sayin' just to get your votes. Untrue. Untrue. I don't pretend I would not like to go to the Senate of the United States. But I do say to you that in comparison with this mighty issue, it is nothing—nothing at all—whether or not Judge Douglas or myself shall ever be heard of again after this night. The Judge tells you I want Negro equality so's I can take to myself a black woman. Good people of Illinois, I'm near fifty years old. I never had a black slave and I never had a black wife; and I reckon I could live another fifty years without either. I do not understand that because I do not want a Negro for a slave I must necessarily want her for a wife. My understanding is that I can just let her alone. I have never had the least apprehension that she would want me to begin with, or that I would need a law to restrain me from wanting her. But as Judge Douglas and his friends seem to think they might need such a law—well, I'd stand by it. Good Lord, but they seem to be in constant fear that some blood-mixing danger lies within them—a danger which only the several State Legislatures and not the Federal Government may rightfully oppose. This bein' the case, may I suggest the Judge be kept at home to organize the Illinois defense. I'll gladly take his place in Washington! *(He pauses.)* Finally, my friends, the Judge says that this democracy can live divided between slave and free if only we all mind our own business. No. It will not be so. As I would not be a slave, so I would not be a master. This is my idea of a democracy. Whatever differs from this, to the extent of the difference, is no democracy. In the black man's right to eat the bread he has earned with his own hands, I say in this democracy he is my equal, the equal of Judge Douglas, or of any man. I cannot compromise with this principle, and yet I see others trying to compromise it with laws and rulings in an effort to put an end to what the Judge calls "this Abolitionist fury." Under the operation of these new laws and regulations the fury has not only *not* ceased, it has constantly augmented. In my opinion it will not cease until a crisis has been reached and passed. A house divided against itself cannot stand. This government cannot endure half slave and half free. God willing, I do not expect the Union to be dissolved. I do not expect the house to fall. But I do expect it will cease to be divided. It must become all one thing or all the other. Either the opponents of slavery will arrest the further spread of it, or its advocates will push it forward. Forward! Until it shall become lawful in all the States! Old as well as new! North as well as South! And if you pursue that course, brother's hand will be raised against brother, and you shall become a slave to the first man you meet with skin fairer than your own!

(The spot dims to black on LINCOLN and picks up SPEED off to one side.)

SPEED: We didn't have our Senators elected by direct vote back in 1858 the way you folks got it today. The people voted, of course, but for electors to the State Legislature. They was the ones cast the final ballots. Kinda like the way you do it now for President. Well, it made for some strange carryin' on. Abe, for example, beat Douglas by 4,085 votes. November two, 1858. Should've been Senator Abraham Lincoln. But that ain't the way it turned out. Seems like the Illinois Legislature wasn't to meet on the matter until January the next year, givin' Douglas plenty of time to—shall we say—use his influence. When all the smoke cleared, it was fifty-four votes to forty-six against Abe, and a damned peculiar smell in the Springfield Statehouse, if you ask me.

(He exits. The spot dims to black.)

SCENE 7

(As the lights come up, ANN—dressed as always—steps out onto the knoll. She carries flowers very much like the ones growing at the base of the tree and carefully arranges them in a basket draped across her arm. After a moment, LINCOLN approaches. He is tired; his head is bowed. He moves slowly toward the tree and stands before it in silence as ANN looks on. It is early in the Spring of 1859.)

LINCOLN: I didn't bring anything for you today, Ann.

ANN: I know all about the election, Abe.

LINCOLN: Not that it seems you need much here. Prairie flowers do right well in the Spring.

ANN: I wouldn't worry about it, Abe. There's more to your destiny than Stephen Douglas.

LINCOLN: I hope you don't mind I come empty-handed. It's just that I...had a need to talk to you.

ANN: You never come empty-handed, Mr. Lincoln. *(He kneels and, as he has done before, works at the garden by the foot of the tree.)* Not to me nor to anyone else. And you never will. This thing is going to pass. You'll see. I know that. Where I am, I know it right well. Why you've got so much in front of you *(He rises and exits.)* if I was to tell you just the half of it, you'd say I was crazy. You hear, Mr. Lincoln? Just the half of it...

(The lights dim to black.)

SCENE 8

(Immediately following. We are in the parlor of the Lincoln house where MARY is pouring tea for JESSE FELL, whom we recognize as the SPEAKER from previous scenes.)

MARY: Just one more cup, Mr. Fell. I don't know what could be keeping Abe. He promised to be home by dinner...

FELL: Serves me right for bargin' in here without an appointment. I just thought it was such good news, why wait on the formalities, if you know what I mean...

MARY: Oh, no. You're absolutely right. It's wonderful news, and Abe will be just thrilled...

(LINCOLN enters, still wearing his hat and coat which he removes during the conversation.)

LINCOLN: About what will I be thrilled, Mary? *(He kisses her cursorily on the cheek and extends his hand to FELL.)* Evening, Jesse. What brings you over this time of day? *(FELL rises in greeting.)*

MARY: Maybe you'd like to sit down, gentlemen. Abe, can I pour you some tea? Mr. Fell's already on his third cup. *(They sit.)*

LINCOLN: Three cups, Jesse? What would keep you in here for three cups of Mary's tea? No offense, my dear. It's just that Jesse usually prefers something stronger.

FELL: Abe, you know I've done right well in real estate...

LINCOLN: Handled some of your work, I think, didn't I?

FELL: Yes. The land by New Salem. Anyway, there's a few of us done real well financially.

LINCOLN: A few of you?

FELL: Judge Davis, Steve Logan, Mr. Delahay...

LINCOLN: Mark Delahay? He's out in Kansas now, isn't he?

FELL: Yes, but folks out there haven't forgotten what you said to Douglas about brother's hand bein' raised against brother.

MARY: I knew that speech would catch fire. That one and the "house divided..."

FELL: You know there's papers in New York made a pamphlet of your speeches, Abe? They say it circulates something wonderful.

LINCOLN: Jesse, what is it you want?

FELL: I want you...that is, we want you...to stand for the Republican nomination for President.

LINCOLN: I thought as much. Favorite son from Illinois...

FELL: Well, we figured you might take the whole shebang.

LINCOLN: Oh, the whole thing, eh, Jesse?

FELL: Well, we figured...

LINCOLN: Beat out Douglas, Seward, maybe even Senator Chase?...and that's not counting any Southerners bound to run.

FELL: Seward and Chase are the only Republicans we got to worry about. If we get the nomination, the South'll probably put up two men at least.

LINCOLN: Breckinridge and Bell...

FELL: More than likely...which is good for us. They'll split the Southern vote and that'll make us all the stronger.

LINCOLN: Jesse, what brings you to think I could beat Douglas, assuming he's the Democratic candidate?

MARY: You beat him in Illinois, Abe. His own state.

LINCOLN: And you'll notice, Ma'am, who's in Washington and whose here in Springfield drinking tea.

FELL: Maybe so, but he won't influence the Electoral College like he did the Illinois Legislature. Not even Steve Douglas blows that hard.

LINCOLN: Don't count your chickens.

FELL: Alright then, let 'em blow. I say the harder he pumps it out, the fewer votes he's goin' to bring home.

MARY: And my Lord, he surely pumps it out.

FELL: Exactly my point. Abe, the man'll stump the country puttin' his foot in his mouth one state after another. And meanwhile there you'll be, sittin' quiet like you do, not causin' any ruckus...

LINCOLN: I won't be silent on the slavery issue, Jesse...

FELL: Now Abe, no one's tryin' to put a bit in your mouth. Just be yourself, that's all we ask.

LINCOLN: *(rising)* Can I have some time to think on it? Talk to Mary? Or have you boys got the buttons printed up already?

FELL: How's a week? Take a good week. *(He rises to go as does MARY.)*

LINCOLN: A week's fine, Jesse.

FELL: Then, by God, we'll run Mr. Douglas right out of a job! *(He offers his hand.)*

LINCOLN: I think you've had too much tea. Goodnight, Jesse. *(They shake hands.)*

FELL: *(to MARY)* Evenin', Mrs. Lincoln.

MARY: Good night, Mr. Fell.

FELL: *(exiting)* So long...Mr. President...

(The lights dim out and reappear on SPEED off to one side.)

SPEED: They didn't have much trouble gettin' Abe past the State Republicans seein' as how the debates had practically made a hero out of him. But the National Convention—that was another ticket. Met in Chicago. Eighteenth of May, 1860, and Abe was anything but the front-runner. Folks come from all across the country, and most of 'em for Bill Seward, former Governor of New York. On the first ballot Abe could only muster 102 votes to Seward's 174—the rest goin' to favorite sons like Chase of Ohio. But Seward was a long way off, there bein' 465 votes available and 233 needed to nominate. It was a horse race right enough. Funny thing was, Abe never showed up in Chicago. When he pledge to run, Fell and the others decided it would be better to keep a low profile, and I must say Abe agreed. Front-runnin' never did sit well on the prairie. So the plan was for Fell to dicker in Chicago and send word back to Abe in Springfield by telegraph. Yessir! After that first ballot, there was dickerin' aplenty, let me tell you. Key man was Chase. If they could win him over, they knew they'd have Seward straddlin' a barrel. Fell sent Abe a wire sayin' Chase would go for a deal, throw his votes to Abe in exchange for Secretary of the Treasury if Abe won the election. Thing was, if Abe beat out Seward for the Republican nomination, he'd need to buy Seward's support in the election, and Seward's people had their eye on the Treasury. "That's the trouble with the world," Abe wired back. "I only got three chestnuts and everyone wants two." They finally settled it by promising the Seward folks Secretary of State. Chase went for the deal and it all come down to the fifth ballot. Glory to God and Jesse Fell.

(The spot follows SPEED as he walks into the LINCOLN parlor in Springfield.)

SCENE 9

(It is now the evening of May 18, 1860. The parlor is dotted with local Lincoln supporters who dance as they await the results of the fifth ballot from Chicago. LINCOLN and MARY circulate among the murmuring guests, freshening drinks and mixing in the small talk. As SPEED walks into the scene the parlor breaks from a frozen tableau to animation and the lights change from shadow to bright. SPEED helps himself to a drink from the tray of a passing maid and makes his way to MARY, center front.)

SPEED: Any word yet?

MARY: Nothing, Joshua. I wish they'd hurry it along.

SPEED: Maybe I oughtta check on that telegraph wire.

MARY: Would you? I'd really appreciate it.

SPEED: *(exiting)* You keep an eye on our boy. I'll be back in a few
    minutes.

(LINCOLN makes his way to MARY.)

LINCOLN: Where's Josh gone to?

MARY: The telegraph office. They certainly are taking their time with
    the fifth ballot. Are you sure you told Jesse to give Mr. Seward what
    we agreed to?

LINCOLN: Yes, Mary.

MARY: And that Chase could keep the Treasury?

LINCOLN: Yes, Mary. Why don't I fetch you another punch?

MARY: You know, I believe I'm more anxious over this than you are.

LINCOLN: I reckon so.

MARY: And how do you explain that, Mr. President?

LINCOLN: *(soberly)* Mr. President. My God, Mary, it almost has the
    ring of death to it.

MARY: Death? Why Abe, it's the most alive, the most...I don't know
    how to say it...vital...yes, vital thing we've ever done.

LINCOLN: Gonna be a long, hard campaign no matter who they pick
    in Chicago.

MARY: What campaign isn't long and hard? The thing is to let Douglas
    blow himself out and let the South divide itself up...

LINCOLN: Yes, I know, Mary. That's what's frightening to me.

MARY: Oh, I don't really think this talk of secession comes to anything. I mean when they find out you're not going to reach down to their plantations and snatch their slaves from them in the dark of night...

LINCOLN: Sometimes a man's fear is a greater enemy than his foe.

MARY: So you'll tell them in your calm and deliberate way, my darling, that they have nothing to fear from you.

LINCOLN: You've an answer for all ills, Mary.

(SPEED reappears with a wire in his hand. The guests begin to crowd around him, murmuring louder.)

MARY: Why of course I have, dear.

LINCOLN: I'm not so sure...

MARY: *(moving to SPEED)* Look! Joshua's back!

(All except LINCOLN gravitate to SPEED who stands on a chair elevated above the rest. LINCOLN remains on the outskirts of the crowd, almost detached from the events.)

SPEED: I have here, good people of Springfield, the results of the fifth ballot in our sister city of Chicago! *(The guests mutter enthusiastically.)* For Mr. Seward...one hundred and one votes. *(a concerned reaction)* For Mr. Chase...no votes! *(a louder reaction)* And for our own Abraham Lincoln...three hundred sixty-four votes *(wild cheering)* and the nomination of the Republican Party for the Office of President of the United States!

(The cheering subsides and the crowd freezes again in tableau. The lights fade but the shadows of the parlour remain visible. LINCOLN alone, now in a spot, moves slowly toward the knoll which comes into view. It is a bright, peaceful night, the moonlight illuminating the spring flowers which grow at the base of the old oak. ANN is already visible. She stands calmly awaiting LINCOLN who emerges from the darkness again into his spot. He carries a new bouquet of prairie flowers, walks to the tree, and begins to plant them.)

ANN: *(as LINCOLN goes about his task)* I've been waiting, Abe...I'd say congratulations, but I know how you feel. Really I do. It isn't going to be easy. I'm not for pretending it's going to be easy. There's going to be a war. We both know that. It's going to be long and bitter and painful. We know that, too. But, Abe, there's no one to get us through it better than you. You may not quite believe that now, but I tell you it's the truth. I've come to know where I am that people end up where they belong the most. You go back to Washington—at least till the fighting's done. And after...well...it won't be long. I promise it won't, and there's so much we have to talk about. *(He rises and walks slowly from the knoll.)* Goodbye, Mr. Lincoln.

(The lights fade down but not out on ANN and up to dim on the tableau in the Springfield parlour. LINCOLN followed by a spot makes his way into the tableau and after he does so, the lights on ANN dim to black. The play is over.)

Notes

Notes

Notes

Notes

Notes

Notes

Notes

Notes